W9-BFP-848

The Complete Book
of Platform Tennis

9/26/77

Mark —
Sorry its delayed but I hope you
enjoy this Book —
Happy Birthday!
Later —
The Schmed

The Complete Book of

PLATFORM TENNIS

Edited by Dick Squires

With a Foreword by Robert A. Brown

Illustrated with photographs,
and line drawings by Laura Duggan

Houghton Mifflin Company Boston   1977

BOOKS BY DICK SQUIRES

How to Play Platform Tennis
The Complete Book of Platform Tennis (Editor)

M 10 9 8 7 6 5 4 3 2

Copyright © 1974 by Richard C. Squires
All rights reserved. No part of this work may
be reproduced or transmitted in any form by any
means, electronic or mechanical, including photocopying
and recording, or by any information storage or retrieval
system, without permission in writing from the publisher.

Library of Congress Cataloging in Publication Data

Squires, Dick.
  The complete book of platform tennis.

  1. Paddle tennis. I. Title.
GV1006.S73   796.34   74-13313
ISBN 0-395-19445-8 ISBN 0-395-25858-8 (pbk.)

Printed in the United States of America

A portion of this book has appeared in *Tennis Magazine*.

Dedication

I believe *The Complete Book of Platform Tennis is* complete! Much of the credit must be given to the contributing authors. Their "secrets" were certainly enlightening to me when I read their manuscripts for the first time. I now have great insight as to how to play against them next time we meet across the net! For that reason, plus, of course, their thorough, thoughtful, and constructive chapters, I gratefully dedicate this book to them.

DICK SQUIRES

Foreword

IF YOU WERE GIVEN the facility to read and put into effect what you were told, you could read *The Complete Book of Platform Tennis* and become a national champion overnight. This book is a collection of advice by experts on every aspect of the game of platform tennis—the serve, serve return, volley, overhead, lob, forehand, the importance of steadiness, screen play, the woman's role, and many other aspects. It provides a reader with an opportunity to learn from the top talent in the game. You can enjoy and gain from reading through the entire book. Or, since it is structured as it is, a certain chapter can be read when it is of particular interest, or as a "refresher."

While the author of each chapter has been asked to instruct on a particular stroke or aspect of the game, you will observe one consistent theme that runs through the book. There is a clear love of the game that pervades much of what is written. Very difficult to describe, this feeling derives from the unique features of platform tennis—the sustained rallies because of the play off the screens, the premium on patience, the importance of teamwork, and that certain spirit about the game that is so pleasant, termed by many as "camaraderie." This atmosphere doesn't seem to exist to the same extent in any other sport. It is this quality and the people that make the game what it is—and this book is written by people who know and love the game and can speak about it with knowledge, experience, and feeling.

One final thought on reading this book on a diversity of subjects by a diversity of writers. Many of the writers are expert platform tennis players. But you will also find that they are excellent writers. In each case, the topic is discussed clearly, the key elements are brought out, the authors explain the "how" and "why," and you leave each chapter with a feeling that you have truly learned something from a "guru" on that subject.

Platform tennis is now beginning to burst at the seams. Although the game was invented over forty-five years ago and national championships have been played for forty years, in the last few years there has been a rapid rise in popularity and public exposure. We believe platform tennis is currently the fastest growing sport in the United States. This book comes at an appropriate time in the blossoming-forth of platform tennis and will be enjoyed and appreciated by not only the veterans in the game but the many newcomers who will be exposed to platform tennis in the years to come.

ROBERT A. BROWN
Former President
American Platform Tennis Association

Contents

Illustrations

Diagrams

Introduction

FOR MANY YEARS people thought of platform tennis as a sport predominantly played by the socially elite behind the carefully clipped hedges of country clubs and affluent estates. To some extent this was an accurate picture. Just a few years ago, however, two of America's current favorite pastimes had this same image. Golf and tennis were originally "sports of kings," and it wasn't until the 1960s that golf became available to and popular with the general public. Tennis didn't break out of its insular surroundings until the 1970s, and who is to say platform tennis won't be the next national sports craze in the 1980s — or sooner?

Today platform tennis has erupted and is destined to be embraced by an immensely receptive public. The game's many unique and appealing features will most assuredly attract millions of Americans who are searching for fun and healthy activities to occupy their increased number of leisure hours. When these people are properly exposed to the fundamentals and enticing attractions of "paddle," they will quickly join the rapidly growing number of avid platform tennis addicts who believe unanimously that there is no better game in the world.

Lately platform tennis has been receiving broad exposure on national television and in magazines, as well as greater coverage in local newspapers. Such publicity helps immensely to promote the timely

The tension of competitive platform tennis is convincingly revealed on John Mangan's face. Note the immutable concentration of referee Bob Brown, President of the American Platform Tennis Association, 1973–1975.

and time-tested attributes of paddle. A historic milestone occurred during the winter of 1973-1974 when, for the *first* time, over 10,000,000 viewers saw a platform tennis tournament on television — CBS's "Sports Spectacular." The event was the Vat Gold Cup, co-sponsored by National Distillers' Munson Shaw Division and the Sea Pines Company. Many other "firsts" were associated with this particular championship, which attracted the top-ranked teams in the country. This event was the first major tournament held in the south, thus shattering the impression that paddle should only be played in cold weather. The winning team, John Mangan and Bob Kingsbury, won an all-expenses-paid trip to Europe (shades of professionalism rearing its ugly head — can Lamar Hunt be too far behind?), and probably most exciting of all, the losing finalists, Steve and Chip Baird, were barely into their twenties.

I hope *The Complete Book of Platform Tennis* will help *all* "paddlers" improve their game. As you read and study the contributions of each author, I believe you will begin to sense the profound affection they have for the game. There is an undeniable respect — almost a reverence — that underlies and permeates their comments. They all love the sport of paddle.

Platform tennis is unique in that it can be (and is!) played outdoors in almost any kind of weather. One of its great attractions is that it *does* offer people living in cold climates a healthy, enjoyable outdoor activity during the wintry months between October and April. However, unlike other racquet games, paddle can also be played outdoors the *year round*. As a fairly active tennis player (still!), I guarantee that playing paddle in the summertime is no more exhausting or enervating than playing tennis on asphalt or cement courts. In addition, platform tennis is a perfect *family game* — easy to play and inexpensive.

Paddle is truly a marvelous activity and form of recreation for *everyone,* including youngsters, middle-aged men and women, and senior citizens. Until about ten years ago, it did seem that only the middle-aged had the patience to play winning platform tennis. Year after year the national champions were invariably "older" businessmen and suburban housewives who usually won out over their younger opponents by sheer tenacity and attrition. Impetuous youths did not seem to possess the maturity or patience to "hang in there." They tried to clobber every ball and overwhelm the opposition. About five years ago I had the temerity to predict it wouldn't be too long before a couple of teen-agers walked off with the Men's and Women's National titles. Very few people agreed with me. Today, few disagree. A new, fresh (and refreshing) breed of youngsters is invading the sport and changing its entire complexion. The "waiting game" is succumbing to the attacking style. The conservative lobber can no longer expect always to win by employing the patience of Job and eventually to triumph by boring his adversaries to death. Youthful speed, aggressive-

Stan Smith, one of the world's top tennis players, also enjoys platform tennis.

ness, agility, forcing shots, boldness, and lightning-fast reflexes are beginning to crush traditional touch tactics.

Platform tennis, despite its innumerable "equalizing elements" (single service, smaller court, screen play), is still very much like the other racquet games in that speed, quick reactions, a "hungry instinct," stamina, determination, and courage are the physical and mental characteristics paying high dividends in tournament play. And obviously most of these traits are more apt to be found in younger athletes. All the "kids" need is the opportunity to be exposed to the game at an early age and to be allowed some time on the courts — then watch out!

Platform tennis is a much *easier* sport to learn than tennis or squash. You don't have to be a beautifully coordinated, natural athlete to play well enough to gain personal satisfaction from the game. On the other hand, it takes just as much skill and practice as tennis requires to become a champion. While "legs and lungs" are not the important factors they are in tennis, there is still a premium on racquet work, ball control, and shot-making. A few years ago I was presenting the merits of paddle to a group of white-haired directors of a well-known tennis club. Following my pitch one gentleman asked, "Mr. Squires, why do you want to take two established sports like tennis and squash, which have proven themselves to be great racquet games, and combine them to create a bastardized offspring that has to be an inferior substitute?" I reminded him that both tennis and squash were "bastardized offsprings" of court tennis and hard racquets. At any rate, his peers apparently shared my enthusiasm for the game. Today their club has four crowded platform tennis courts — and they are considering building more.

Like any other bona fide racquet and ball sport, platform tennis has unique strokes and strategies. While there is usually no big payoff on power, finesse is certainly rewarded. Stan Smith, generally accepted as one of the top tennis players in the world today, plays and really enjoys paddle when he's away from the tour. He believes it hones his reflexes and net play. But as great a tennis player as he is, he and Rod Laver would get "creamed" by a couple of good paddlers. Platform tennis possesses its own distinctive nuances and subtleties. Easy to learn, but difficult to master.

Over a two-year period, Dick Squires played forty-three exhibitions
to inaugurate new court installations. Such instructional demonstrations
help assure the popularity of paddle in areas that previously had little
exposure to the sport.

Platform tennis is a wonderfully *exciting* game *to watch* as well as to play. Rallies are extended and varied. The single service alone offers a tantalizing and suspenseful element — especially at a crucial point of any important championship match. Frequently all four players are at the net together and the action-packed play and rapid-fire volleying is something to behold. A top-ranked platform tennis player has to have as complete a game as a tennis player. Though he does not have to be the athlete (from the standpoint of stamina and conditioning) that a circuit-playing tennis star is, his overall racquet work and reflexes must be just as sound and versatile in all categories of stroke production. There is no way today's paddlers can rely on one outstandingly awesome stroke — one ultimate weapon that works practically every time on a platform tennis court. There are too many leveling factors. The platform tennis gallery, therefore, is usually watching tense and close matches. A championship paddle match is easily understood and beautiful to view.

A rooftop court in mid-Manhattan. The Town Tennis Club is an excellent example of places platform tennis courts can be installed. Above, Dick Squires (l.) and Hammering Herb FitzGibbon (r.) playing an APTA–sponsored exhibition for the press.

Platform tennis can have a *positive* influence on one's tennis game by improving accuracy and anticipation at the net, volleying, and confidence. However, because of the totally different "feel" between making contact with a sponge-rubber ball and a solid wooden paddle, it would be rather difficult to play platform tennis in the morning and regular tennis in the afternoon of the same day. You would experience real problems in controlling the ball. I do know, however, that you can play paddle one day and tennis the next with little or no difficulty.

In addition, the platform tennis court is an absolutely perfect training ground for very young children to learn the basics of tennis and platform tennis. In my opinion, parents make a serious mistake when they shove their offspring onto the regular tennis court at an age when they are too small and frail to return the ball across the net. The court must look like a football field to them! (The patient teaching tennis professional usually plunks very young pupils on the *service line,* at any rate, when teaching ground strokes, so they at least have a fifty-fifty chance of returning the ball.) On the other hand, children seem to be able to relate to the smallness of the paddle court. They're not overwhelmed by the size, and I have personally seen some amazing rallies take place between four children who are just about the same height as the net posts.

Despite the positive appeals of platform tennis, the mere installation of courts does *not* automatically insure their instant popularity and use. Even though the game is relatively easy to learn, a beginning player, lacking knowledge of basic fundamentals and strategy, can quickly become disenchanted and frustrated. It is therefore very important that some form of instruction be offered to potential paddlers wherever and whenever courts are built. An orientation program explaining the game's basic strokes and strategy is essential. Ideally the program should consist of an exhibition/clinic staged by four good players. Such an inaugural demonstration should be supported by a planned program of organized tournaments, additional clinics, and social activities centered around paddle, and equipment should be readily available for interested people. Once unknowing individuals are properly exposed to the correct fundamentals the sport will sell itself to its participants — and there is no one more "hooked" on a game than the paddler!

Dick Squires (r.) introduces Mike Gibson, Wimbledon's famous tennis referee, to platform tennis. Mike believes paddle will one day become a very popular sport in the United Kingdom.

Platform tennis *is* a great racquet and ball sport to be played and enjoyed by any and everyone. It has come to represent virtually a way of life for many of its 150,000 aficionados. Paddle's appeals are irrefutable and have been *proven* over a period of approximately a half century. The current rage is, therefore, not just a passing fad. The world is ready for the timely attractions of this marvelous game. It has been predicted by even the most conservative that by 1984 over 1,000,000 people will be playing this great sport on some 20,000 courts. This meteoric growth and spread of platform tennis is today merely the ground swell compared to the tidal wave that must come during the next few years. Paddle is, indeed, a mere single serve away from becoming America's next major participation sport.

DICK SQUIRES

John P. Ware, former President of the American Platform Tennis
Association (1961–1963), is certainly well qualified to write about the
history of the game. Married to one of Fessenden S. Blanchard's
daughters, Molly, he is fully aware of what really happened in the late
1920s when the first court was installed. He has been brought up on
platform tennis and has contributed a great deal to the orderly growth
and organization of the sport. Another love is yachting. He coauthored
with Roger F. Duncan *A Cruising Guide to the New England Coast*.

1. | JOHN P. WARE

A Brief History of Platform Tennis

IN LATE OCTOBER of 1776, on the eve of the Battle of White Plains, footweary American soldiers were seen dragging their cannon and supplies northward along Old Army Road in Scarsdale, New York. They were marching within a bayonet's toss of the birthplace, a century and a half later, of what was to become quite a different battle scene — not one of shot and shell but one of a competitive sport using bat and ball.

Often the birth of a sport "just happens." Whoever invents it does so without any goal in mind and leaves no records, resulting in origins ill defined and subject to question. The history of platform tennis is an exception.

Platform tennis owes its origin to playground paddle tennis, which was conceived in 1898 at Albion, Michigan. Young Frank P. Beal, barred from the Albion College campus on which his older brother played tennis, ended his frustration and founded paddle tennis in his own backyard. In space not over one quarter the size of a tennis court, with tape discarded by the caretaker of the college courts, some chicken wire for a net, paddles made from a one-inch maple plank, and some old tennis balls, Beal played the first game of paddle tennis. Later, as associate minister of the Judson Memorial Church in Washington Square, New York, he was faced with a recreational problem for the boys of the neighborhood and remembered his invention. He laid out similar courts on the floor of the church gymnasium. Reverend Beal soon became Recreation Chairman of the Community Councils of New York, and his game was played on the streets and playgrounds, providing children with a sport that taught them the rudiments of tennis in a small area and at a minimum expense. The game flourished and the United States Paddle Tennis Association was founded in 1923.

"It wasn't until we stumbled on paddle tennis that we found what we really wanted." The "we" refers to the late Fessenden S. Blanchard and James K. Cogswell, co-founders of the newer version of the game — platform tennis. What they wanted on that rather dismal day in their hometown of Scarsdale in late November of 1928 was a new sport, a red-blooded game offering a stiff workout in fresh air during winter months. The two suburbanites had been grousing to each other about the unhappy outlook for the fall and winter weekends and the prospect of many days of muddy grounds and slushy snow before the tennis season dawned again. Squash had to be played indoors; they wanted to be outdoors. Family walks might have eased their con-

The street version of paddle.

sciences but certainly would not have satisfied their competitive instincts.

In many ways these co-founders were in the same position as Britain's Major Walter C. Wingfield when he originated modern lawn tennis. Like Wingfield, these gentlemen were all-round sportsmen, and athletic games were among their hobbies: they wanted a sociable but strenuous out-of-doors game, and to find one they were willing to experiment on their own property. So the two men, with Cogswell as "chief engineer," built a solid wooden platform on a strip of land of the Cogswell estate high over the corner of Old Army and Ardsley Roads, convinced that they'd have some fun on that platform — either with deck tennis, volleyball, or some other sport. As will be noted, the size and shape of that strip of land helped make the game what it is today. By the end of 1928 the first platform was completed with dimensions of 48' x 20' and marked out for badminton and deck tennis. The court could not be made any wider than twenty feet without raising the entire structure over a troublesome rock, and at forty-eight feet in length anything longer would have made the platform jut out like a springboard from a cliff.

The two zealots soon discovered that this unsheltered location did not offer a good game of badminton and that deck tennis was not for them. One day, however, the undaunted Cogswell appeared on his court with some paddle tennis equipment he had purchased in a New York store. The paddles were made of three-ply, resin-bonded birch, shaped like a rectangle, and rounded at the corners with a solid grooved face. Each was 14¾ inches long and 7¾ inches wide, with a weight of about 8½ ounces. The balls, closely resembling those of today, consisted of solid, slow-bouncing sponge rubber approximately 2½ inches in diameter and almost exactly the same size as a tennis ball.

Keeping these balls in the court posed a problem, so around the platform went chicken wire of two-inch mesh stapled to two-by-four uprights eight feet high. Blanchard and Cogswell also decided that the 44' x 20' badminton measurements were better for adult platform play than the 39' x 18' measurements used in the original form of paddle tennis, since the shortness of the original platform provided a scant two feet between the back line and back wire.

It was the following event, however, that helped to "make the game." During an early match, one of Blanchard's opponents hit a ball that landed in the court, then flew up and stuck in the back wire. "It's still in play!" cried the fiery Blanchard, an intrepid improviser when it came to rules. He ran behind the fence and gave the ball a terrific swat, sending it back into his opponent's court. Catching the spirit of the moment, Blanchard's partner fought off the attacks of their adversaries until Blanchard made his way back onto the court. At last they won the point. After deep discussion, the following rule was accepted: players could take the ball off the back or side wiring, provided the ball had first bounced inside the court's official playing lines and before it had hit the platform deck a second time. This new feature of the game produced prolonged and exciting rallies. Furthermore, screen play tended to neutralize the sheer power of the overhead smash during play, since the hardest-hit ball could be rather effortlessly returned off the wires.

By 1932, other innovations had been accepted. Cogswell rebuilt his platform within an enlarged 60′ x 30′ area, using concrete blocks to support deck boards of Douglas fir spaced slightly apart to permit drainage of rain and snow. The net was lowered to two feet, ten inches at the center strap, with back and side wires raised to their present twelve-foot height. By introducing the one-service rule, a fair balance of advantage between server and receiver was achieved. The domination of the server, so prevalent in lawn tennis, was fortunately avoided. With these notable exceptions, the standard rules of tennis apply.

From such simple beginnings the game grew in favor. Inquisitive neighbors along Old Army Road began dropping by the Cogswells' to see the game they affectionately called paddle. Soon the hosts had to provide benches and a room full of football robes. To see and then to play was to become converted. The game soon developed, and still does develop, an unusually warm spirit of conviviality among its adherents. "Tea after paddle" served by Mrs. Cogswell became a tradition. Few groups of sportsmen were more ardently dedicated to a game than the original group of players — the "Old Army Athletes." One of these "athletes," the late author Frederick Lewis Allen, considered it "one of the best games ever invented." One of their group made a lasting contribution to the game during its formative stages.

Fessenden S. Blanchard (l.) and James K. Cogswell.

A paddle match in the early days.

For several years players had been plagued by irregular bounces coming off the loosely strung backstop and side wires. The founders knew that platform tennis could never become a game of skill as long as the luck of the bounce prevailed. Donald K. Evans of Scarsdale provided the answer. In 1934 he created a design making it possible to stretch the one-inch wire mesh from the top to the bottom well inside of the uprights but not touching them. Adjustable tension bars also helped to provide a uniform bounce for balls caroming off any one of the court's four screens.

Looking back, Blanchard claimed that "it was the members of this Old Army Athletes group of twenty-five to thirty families who were the real pioneers in putting platform tennis on the map in ever-widening communities. Some of them erected platforms at their homes or summer places. Visitors from other towns came, saw, and were conquered."

The first club in America to be "conquered" was the Fox Meadow Tennis Club in Scarsdale. The oldest tennis club in Westchester

Earle Gatchell (l.) and Fessenden S. Blanchard.

County, it was founded in 1883 and began with two tennis courts and twenty members. The construction of a platform court in 1931 and a second court in 1934 saved Fox Meadow from certain bankruptcy during the Great Depression, as the club began to attract more members with year-round sports activities. With such an early interest and with the many contributions of its members to the sport, in addition to an impressive array of nine paddle courts, the Fox Meadow Tennis Club rightfully has been called the Forest Hills of platform tennis.

In 1934, platform tennis started to come of age. Blanchard and Cogswell were busy promoting their new sets of plans and specifications to all comers. A special "Non-Skid Surface" was developed by Richard Grant of the Tremont Place Paddle Tennis Club of Orange, New Jersey, by sprinkling fine beach sand onto the deck as the traditional green paint was applied. Henry B. Eaton, a former president of Fox Meadow, created a portable platform, amazingly priced at $500, that could be easily transported, erected in a day, and laid on top of existing tennis courts without damaging them. Clubs like the Manursing Island Club of Rye, the Field Club of Greenwich, the Ardsley Racquet and Swimming Club, and the Bronxville Field Club snapped up these courts from Gates Sports Platform Company. Courts were beginning to spring up in such cities as Boston; Springfield, Massachusetts; New Haven; Philadelphia; Cleveland; Chicago; Danville, Virginia; and Los Angeles. The game needed an official governing association.

Due in considerable degree to the leadership of the late John C. Ten Eyck, Jr., of the Manursing Island Club of Rye, New York, the American Paddle Tennis Association was formed in November 1934. The charter members were the Field Club of Greenwich, Connecticut, the Fox Meadow Tennis Club, and the Manursing Island Club. Ten Eyck, Warren A. Ransom, and Grenville S. Sewell represented Manursing, Foster M. Hampton represented the Field Club, and Fessenden S. Blanchard represented Fox Meadow. The original purpose of the Association was and still is to standardize rules and equipment, to promote the popularity of the game, and to sponsor tournaments.

Tournaments and platform tennis were made for each other; they both thrive on sociability and competition. The Old Army Athletes even had an informal "marital championship" in 1930 with sixteen teams — husband-wife pairs only. There was a penalty of one point for each time a husband criticized the play of his wife, and vice versa. The judges had to listen carefully to detect any faint signs of sarcasm when sweet remarks seemed somewhat overdone. The first formal tournament on record was held at Scarsdale in December 1931. Forty-two teams competed in the championship, which was won by Fessenden Blanchard and Earle Gatchell, who defeated Randolph Compton and James Hynson.

The variety of tournaments in platform tennis is almost as broad as the ages of those who enter them. There are parent-child, husband-wife, junior, senior, senior-veteran (for men over sixty years of age), and special tournaments called "scrambles" in which good players are carefully paired with those not so proficient so that all can have a go at the trophy. The scrambles idea was inspired by Kenneth Ward, one of the game's most ardent spokesmen, and instituted by Oscar "Oz" Moore at their Manursing Island Club in 1942. One day they were heard complaining:

"I have the worst luck in these scrambles tournaments," said Ken. "I never seem to draw anybody who is any good. Why sometimes my partners haven't ever seen a paddle. Of course, if I did get anyone that was any good, they'd all be suspicious."

"I'm the same way," replied Oz. "I never get a good partner either. I'm always out of luck too."

"Let's compare notes," suggested Ken. "Who did you draw last year?"

"You!" cried Oz.

Ward was president of the APTA at the time.

The first "national" championships were organized by the Association in 1935 and held at Fox Meadow. Men's singles, men's and women's doubles, and mixed doubles were staged. After three years singles matches were dropped because the combination of a net and rebound screen sport is best suited to team play. These major tournaments developed growing interest in platform tennis, but the special exhibition matches really took this new winter way of life into distant places. Some of the outstanding athletes who participated in these matches included Charles O'Hearn of Yale football fame, Clifford Sutter, Tulane's national intercollegiate tennis winner, John Cookman,

The younger Baird brothers challenge John Mangan and Bob Kingsbury.

Yale's intercollegiate champion at squash racquets, and Ben Ticknor, a Harvard gridiron great. In more recent years such tennis stars as Stan Smith, Chuck McKinley, Clark Graebner, and Gene Scott have been bitten by the "paddle bug." Former U.S.L.T.A. champions Frank Guernsey and Donald McNeill also became National APTA doubles winners in 1953 and 1954.

By 1963 the American Platform Tennis Association (the name was changed from American Paddle Tennis Association in 1950 to better reflect the nature of the game) consisted of seventy member clubs and an estimated 25,000 people playing the game. Ten years later APTA's President Robert Brown reported that the "Association, with its 265 member clubs, sanctioned a record nine National champion-ships and another thirty-nine regional tournaments. These are held not only in the northeast, the long-time bastion of platform tennis, but in far places like Hilton Head, South Carolina, Chicago, Cleveland, Denver. We estimate there now exist from 2500 to 3000 courts with over 150,000 devotees of all ages engaging in the sport. At our present rate of growth, that last figure will climb to a million players by early in the next decade! Courts are even springing up in Japan, Germany, Italy, Puerto Rico, Canada, and Poland."

Before he died co-founder Blanchard expressed the feelings of all aficionados of this marvelous sport when he said, "Every weekend when Jimmy and I visit Fox Meadow, we are visibly reminded of what platform tennis has meant to our community, and we get a real 'kick.' We know what it has meant to us and to our friends. We know also that there are hundreds, even thousands of communities like ours who can and will have the same fun we have had."

As for the future of the game, Mrs. Rawle Deland, daughter of James Cogswell, tells us, "For years the game was played mostly at clubs and private homes. Now it's going back to the public, back to the parks and playgrounds where it originally came from."

Richard K. Hebard has won more National titles than any other man who ever lifted a paddle. Eight times he annexed the National Men's Doubles crown, three times with Frederick B. Walker, two with James M. Carlisle, and three with Alexander H. Carver, Jr. Twice he was a finalist. He also won three National Mixed Doubles titles with Madge Beck, once with Ruth Chalmers, and once with Charlotte Lee, and he was twice a finalist. Through the years he continues to prove that paddle can be played competitively for most of one's life. He was National Senior Men's Doubles Champion (age 50 or over) in 1960 and 1961 (with Walter H. Close), 1965 (with Sidney Sweet), and in 1970 with "Zan" Carver. In all, he's won seventeen U.S. platform tennis titles! He was also a very fine tennis player and as a scrawny fourteen-year-old (1928) he won the National Boys' Tennis Singles title. Truly the relaxed, classic stylist, he will undoubtedly stash away several more National Championships in the Senior Veterans' (age 60 and over) category before he hangs up his paddle. In 1965 the American Platform Tennis Association acknowledged his prodigious accomplishments by presenting him with their esteemed Honor Award and the green jacket that acclaims him a "Champion of Champions."

2. | RICHARD K. HEBARD

How the Game Has Changed

I HAVE PLAYED with and against most of the leading platform tennis players of the last twenty years. Twenty years ago platform tennis winners were those able to defend effectively off the wires and gain the advantage if they were blessed with a forceful, aggressive net game.

Before 1954, for example, the lob was strictly a defensive shot, but today it is used as a strong and efficient *offensive* weapon. It has often been said that the best defense is a good offense, and platform tennis is no exception to this maxim. Today, because of the "attack" strategy, platform tennis has become a completely new and different game. The name of the game is *attack*. When there are four aggressive players in competition, defense is important, but the team that consistently gains and retains the net position with offensive tactics eventually wins the match.

All top-flight players should have good ground strokes, be "sound" off the wires with an offensive lob and an occasional drive, and possess a strong, reliable serve. The team that attacks an opponent's serve, however, and gets to the net to make a winner off the opponent's first volley ultimately wins. Aggressive, effective doubles teams today will charge the net against an opponent's serve no matter how good the serve!

No longer do two men always storm the net together. Frequently the receiver hits and then blitzes while his partner remains in the back court. If the receiver does not hit a forceful return of service, his partner must be ready to salvage the point with a deep, high lob, thereby giving his attacking teammate time to retreat and wait for another opportunity to charge the net. Sometimes it is better for the receiver to stay back while his partner advances to the net. This is a variation of the blitz and often surprises the opposition. Naturally the success of this tactic depends largely on how well the service is returned. The paramount objective of either net-rushing strategy is always for a team to gain the commanding position at net.

When four highly proficient paddlers are competing against each other, a point can frequently take two or three minutes to be decided. Consequently the ball can cross the net as many as fifty or sixty times. Top players today have really become very efficient at keeping the ball in play, and the steady, prolonged exchanges provide average players and enthusiastic watchers alike with tournament play that is fraught with excitement and varied, frenzied rallies. The games are action-

Younger players now play a more aggressive game than the older paddlers.

packed and court positions can often vary and reverse as each duo watches, catlike, to grab an opportunity to steal the net for the put-away shot and an earned point.

Before the 1960s a player seldom went back to the wires to retrieve a ball hit between him and his partner. Such a shot was considered unplayable and, therefore, a point for the opposition. Today this is by no means true. If a ball gets by the team at net, one of the two players will race back feeling he has an excellent chance to return the ball off the wires by making a saving lob. The better players do this time and time again effortlessly and confidently. Thus many fine, hard-hitting players in big tournaments today find it difficult to score points by sheer force. In addition, present techniques in the form of aggressive wire play have extended the length of the rallies. Twenty years ago there was no such thing as "aggressive wire play." Today the game demands more finesse, some patience, and especially the ability to sense the right time for the offensive shot or move resulting in an outright winner or a forced error.

It is difficult to forecast how platform tennis will further develop and change in the future, but it certainly has undergone a tremendous new look during the last twenty years. Some of the best players in the game today — most of them are good tennis players with "big" serves — cannot apply enough spin on the ball to force their opponents into making a defensive return off their deliveries. A big server will eventually put the ball into the wires, and an adroit adversary can make a great offensive shot from what really was a good, well-placed, hard serve. In other words, *too good* a serve can provide the opposition with a "fat" setup. One wonders, therefore, how much the service can be improved over the next twenty years!

I believe the best tournament players of the early years were hitting the ball just as hard as the current crop is and were serving and defending about as well, but they were never the attackers of the present era. The old theory was to play a "waiting" game. The player with a technically sound serve had an advantage (as in tennis) over his opponent. The receiver, after putting the ball into play, waited for the opportune moment to attack and win a point. Today there is no waiting. The team that is aggressive from the very outset of the match — attacking the opponent's serve with consistency — will invariably win.

Editor's Note: The ultimate in aggressive play was awesomely displayed during the finals of the recently completed 1974 National Men's Doubles. The new champions, Herb FitzGibbon and John Beck, played the most offensive paddle I have ever seen. They literally "crushed" *every* return of serve, seldom threw up lobs unless caught way out of position, cut off balls whenever possible before they bounded into the screens, slashed their returns off the wires, and when one of them was returning serve the other was up at the net. Furthermore, Beck, a left-hander, played the deuce side of the court. In other words, they seemingly were breaking all the tried and traditional rules in the paddle book. They were employing *tennis* tactics on a platform tennis court and not only "getting away with it," but they were successfully overpowering and intimidating their opponents to death.

While their rather unorthodox tactics might herald a new style of play — with greater emphasis on all-out power — it is well to keep in mind that Beck and FitzGibbon have played as a team for over five years. During this period they have experimented with different shots and formations. Once they thought they had a winning approach they stayed with it and diligently practiced what was required to keep it all together, namely, the ability to blast every return of serve and still be able to realize a *high percentage* of winners or forced errors. It was only through hard work, a good deal of practice, and staying with this somewhat unconventional approach under competitive, tournament conditions that they finally did succeed. In effect, they did *not* ignore the fundamental precepts of winning paddle. What they did do on that chilly March afternoon was to take a giant step forward by being able to hit the ball harder and still keep it in the court a higher percentage of the time than most people ever thought was possible.

Beginners should *not* model their games after Beck and FitzGibbon. While learning, the name of the game is patience, ball placement, and control. Only after one realizes this and develops a high degree of skill in these areas can he attempt to become more offensive and hit more forcing shots. John and Herb merely showed what *can* be accomplished, but only after many years of playing together and working on a particular style that was right for them.

In the 1974 fortieth annual National Men's Doubles, John Beck (l.) and Herb FitzGibbon show the aggressive net play that enabled them to annex the coveted crown.

Let me dwell a moment on the number of good teams that competed in the major tournaments twenty years ago and the teams of today. In the midfifties the National Men's Doubles Championship draw consisted of 80 to 90 teams, with 10 to 12 good pairs and 3 to 4 outstanding ones. Practically everyone could predict which teams would face each other in the semifinals. Today, the same tournaments will have between 120 to 130 teams, with 35 to 40 good teams and 18 to 20 truly outstanding teams. Any one of several teams can "get hot," ignite, upset some favored teams, and walk off with the title. A marked increase in the number of participants and in the number of superior players has necessitated qualifying rounds for national championships in both the men's and women's categories. This shows great growth and progress.

Another major change that is especially noticeable to us "old-timers" is that, at long last, the younger athletes are attracted to the sport of platform tennis. One of the appealing features of paddle is that it is not as demanding as tennis. The platform tennis court is much smaller and is primarily a doubles game, so the participants do not have as much court to cover. Granted, the rallies are longer, but as you get older you get smarter and learn to conserve your energy. An "old man" of forty, therefore, can really "hang in there" against "kids" half his age. This fact alone makes platform tennis truly unique.

As in any bona fide racquet game, however, speed and reflexes still pay off — especially today where play and strategy are so oriented toward offense. The attacking style has actually done much to attract the youngsters to the paddle court. Years ago, when their parents played on the weekends at their local clubs, youngsters saw a great deal of repetitious lobbing and defensive shot-making. To them the sport must have looked pretty boring and simple. They wanted more action! With the advent of more aggressive tactics (primarily instigated a few years ago by the younger players), youths who previously had played either squash or tennis year-round started playing platform tennis. Their more reckless and all-out, aggressive style has contributed immensely toward making paddle a better game.

Platform tennis courts are springing up everywhere. Schools and colleges, military bases, municipalities, resorts and land developments, even major hotels and apartment complexes have installed courts. Commercial "Pay for Play" centers are becoming more prevalent and profitable. Many courts have been recently constructed abroad, so international competition is probably not far off.

Since platform tennis began its present phenomenal rate of expansion, the equipment manufacturers have started to come up with better and newer products. Today there are more balls of varying weights, degrees of hardness or softness, and quality than in the past. As in nearly all racquet sports the lack of consistency and quality control in manufacturing is a constant concern of players as well as the officials of the American Platform Tennis Association. Undoubtedly the continued growth and development of the sport will encourage additional manufacturers to enter the production field and eventually design a first-rate ball. There are also more platform tennis paddle models to choose from today. Paddle weights vary considerably and superior production techniques and better grades of lumber are now used.

New court designs have been introduced and accepted. The all-wooden, planked courts of yesteryear are rapidly being replaced by all-metal courts or combination exterior plywood solid decks with steel superstructures. While these courts cost substantially more than the traditional wooden ones, over the long run court owners pay far less maintenance expenses, have a structure that lasts much longer, and get overall superior, truer playing characteristics. In addition the screens around today's courts are uniform and players can more or less gauge the bounce of the ball correctly once it is hit into the wires. Some years ago this was not true, since many wires were loose and sagging while others were too tight. Players had to be extremely flexible to adapt themselves to constantly changing court conditions.

Now relegated to the dubious status of the "canny veteran," I look back on the "good old days" and fondly remember when just a few of us "owned" this wonderful sport. It was a comfortable feeling. We knew all the people by their first names and also knew exactly how to play against them! Today a new crop of fresh, youthful faces is appearing on the paddle scene to challenge the perennial tournament winners. And, although I say it rather reluctantly, I have to admit they have made platform tennis a more interesting and exciting game.

3. | DICK SQUIRES

Attire and Equipment

ONE OF THE VERY appealing features of platform tennis is its informality. So far no imaginative sportswear firm has created and marketed an "official" uniform for paddle, and men and women alike "do their thing" when it comes to playing attire. You see everything from baggy tweeds with die-cut hearts sewn on the knees or rear to colorfully embroidered designs on durable corduroys. Many women wear stretch pants or kilts with leotards. These outfits are topped off by layers of sweaters if the weather is very cold. The key to paddle garb is to be comfortable and *warm*. Don't wear anything that binds or inhibits your swing or movement. A few of the newcomers to the game have had the temerity to don track or tennis warm-up suits, but they quickly discover their clothes are not considered *de rigueur* by the inveterate paddlers! In warmer climates, regular tennis togs suffice, but some court surfaces are fairly rough and it is a good idea to wear cotton slacks to protect your knees should you slip.

The spectator watching top-notch platform tennis for the first time during the cold winter months is always amazed to see the competitors start peeling off the layers of sweaters until they are down to a cotton T-shirt or turtleneck. While the sedentary gallery shivers in their overcoats, scarfs, and earmuffs, the competing players are glistening with perspiration.

The flexible double-knit fabrics and fast-drying fabrics seem to be the most practical garments for platform tennis. Perhaps one day, as more and more people take up paddle, some official playing uniform will be designed and developed, but I personally hope that's still a few years off. I prefer the lack of standardization in dress and the carefree, almost nonchalant attitude toward what is worn for play. It adds to the fun.

At this time only one athletic shoe distributor (Sports Beconta) has designed a sneaker specifically for platform tennis. This features a very durable sole, extra protection around the toe (for the servers who slide the rear foot in the process of making their delivery), and a somewhat higher back (to offer added protection to the Achilles' tendon).

Several companies manufacture and merchandise APTA-approved balls. Most of them look quite similar and all of them still leave something to be desired in durability and uniformity of bounce and quality. However, I do not know of any racquet and ball sport (including tennis) where one ball pleases *all* the players. The "big hitters" want a livelier ball and the subtle, "touch" players desire a slower or mushier one. The sponge-rubber ball, approximately the same diameter ($2\frac{1}{2}''$) as a tennis ball, is orange in color and somewhat heavier. It is not a pressurized ball, which is probably the main reason for the heaviness of the paddles. The traditional orange color seems to be the best color in winter against a snowy white background. It is my personal judgment, however, that a bright yellow ball would be better for night paddle under the lights as well as for following the fast rallies on color television.

Current ball distributors include Marcraft, Eagle Rubber, Sports Beconta, General Sportscraft, and Barr. Balls cost between $.75 and $1.00 each and will last almost as long as tennis balls (better players change at the end of a set or two, while "duffers" might use a ball for several outings).

There are at the present time three manufacturers of paddles that have been approved by the APTA; Marcraft (Autograph, Bantam, Marc, and Dick Squires Signature models), Dalton (Skill, P-I, and I-O models) and Cragin-Simplex (I and A-I models). The heavier weights run around eighteen to nineteen ounces and the medium and lighter models fifteen to seventeen ounces.

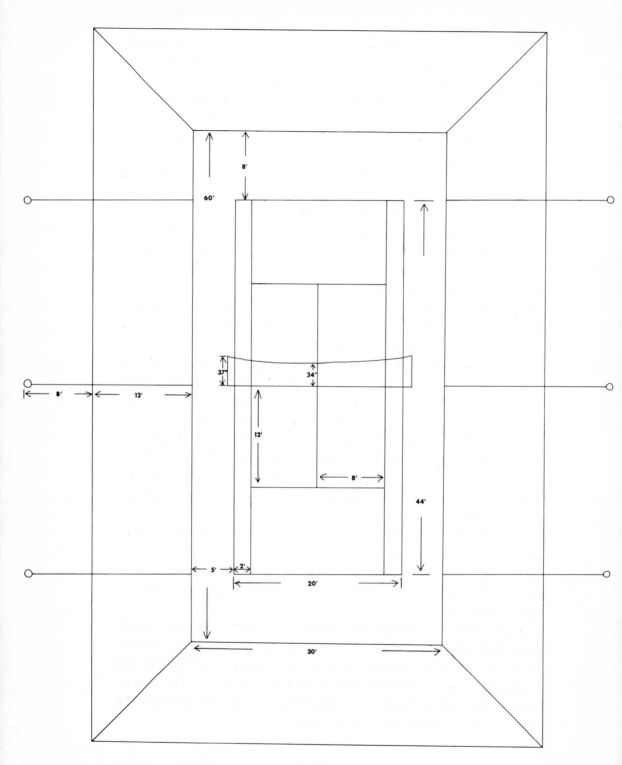

Dimensions of official platform tennis court.

These particular paddles are oval in shape and consist of a perforated rock-maple-plywood hitting surface bound with a metal frame. As the sport continues to grow, new paddle concepts will inevitably be developed, i.e., aluminum, plastic, fiber glass, etc. Present paddles retail from $18.00 to $32.00, and all of them, with minimum care, should last for many years. You do not have as wide a choice of grips as are available in tennis racquets, but there is no reason why any paddle grip cannot be either built up, reduced, or shaped to your particular liking. You can do this yourself, or your local sporting goods dealer or club professional can be helpful.

One final word about paddles and the confusion that usually occurs when the game has just been introduced into a new area. Many unknowing beginners will purchase paddles from sporting goods retailers that are *not* platform tennis paddles at all! They are paddleball paddles. The main difference is that the paddleball paddles do not have the drilled holes in the *center* of the paddle face. In platform tennis the holes play an important, dual role — they reduce the wind resistance and also tend to "bite" the ball and provide the hitter with some feel and control.

One final piece of equipment that I feel naked without is a platform tennis glove. Made of especially thin leather and having wool on the back side, these gloves provide warmth to the player's hands as well as a surer feel and grip on the paddle handle. Many golfers believe they play golf better with a golf glove than they do without one. I feel the same way about a paddle glove. There are several on the market today that generally sell for $10.00.

Platform tennis has been described as a sport played with "dimestore instruments." When compared to the much greater investment one has to make in equipment if he is a skier, golfer, tennis or squash player, or sailor, certainly paddle represents a very inexpensive sport. The playing area or arena, however, is another matter. The original court was built for around $400 in 1928. Today the courts cost in the neighborhood of between $11,000 and $18,000 — which, needless to say, is a pretty fancy neighborhood!

There are basically three types of APTA-approved courts, and probably nine out of ten courts built today *include* lights for extended night play.

1. The so-called traditional, all-wooden planked court. The main problem with this classic design is that the supply of specified good quality 2 x 6–inch Douglas fir, vertical grain, kiln-dried lumber is becoming scarce. Many "fly-by-night" gypsy builders or do-it-yourselfers have purchased plans and inferior lumber (to save money) and built courts that look twenty years old after a single winter. A properly installed all-wooden court, however, is perfectly satisfactory and will provide the court owner with many years of pleasure — although the cost of annual maintenance can run as much as $1000. These courts are priced at the low end of the cost scale.

2. Recently modular courts have been winning widespread popularity in the paddle world. The solid (not planked) deck is constructed of exterior plywood panels. The playing surface is pitched slightly for drainage. The superstrucure is of durable rectangular steel tubing, which can better withstand the tremendous tension of the wires without bowing or cracking. These courts are trim and attractive in appearance and offer the promise of lower upkeep. A completely installed court on a normal site costs approximately $14,000. A heated deck can be included as an option for an additional nominal cost.

3. All-aluminum or combination aluminum decking (extruded planks) and wooden superstructure courts are also becoming more popular. Being of metal construction, these courts preclude the necessity of periodically having to replace rotted or warped wooden planks. Priced between $14,000 and $18,000 (with a heated deck), depending on whether they are the combination of aluminum decking and wooden superstructure or all-aluminum, these courts undoubtedly in the long run are less costly than the all-wooden courts because of their relative permanence and lower maintenance expense.

As platform tennis expands into the south and warmer climates where snow and ice are not factors, and as it is played year-round, there will often be no need to elevate the courts on concrete piers. In cases in which multiple courts are going to be installed side by side, ground level paddle courts will be constructed. They will not be raised but will look like minitennis courts with the 60 x 30 foot playing area made of concrete or asphalt slabs with probably some type of soft, cushiony coating for a top surface. The superstructure will either be lagged in around the slab or installed on ground level piers surrounding the periphery of the playing area.

The American Platform Tennis Association, c/o The Fox Meadow Club, Wayside Lane, Scarsdale, New York 10583, will be glad to offer any interested parties a list of approved equipment manufacturers and court builders. Since by far the greatest investment is in the court, it is wise and prudent to deal only with experienced, reputable court installers. The professionals, while perhaps quoting somewhat higher prices than nonprofessionals, will, in the long run, save the court owners a great deal of money and grief. There truly is an "art" to building a proper platform tennis court, and a court improperly constructed is worse than no court at all!

John F. Mangan is thirty-eight years old, a Rye, New York, resident, and commuting New York City stockbroker. John was National Men's Doubles champion (with Bob Kingsbury) in 1972 and 1973. He also won the National Mixed Doubles crown in 1970 with Suzy Harris. An excellent tennis player as well, he possesses one of paddle's most devastating strokes — the topspin forehand drive. An amazingly agile player for his size, he is known as a fiery competitor, toughest under pressure but at all times a fine sportsman. While winning nearly every other major invitational tournament, John also has his hands full off the court. He and his attractive wife Patricia have six children.

4. | JOHN F. MANGAN

The Forehand

Introduction: The fundamental and most often used stroke in platform tennis is the forehand. For all the variety of strokes employed when playing paddle, and the individual preferences players develop for particular, favorite shots, it is significant to note that, almost without exception, all experienced players, especially tournament-toughened competitors, agree the *forehand* is the single *most important stroke* in the game. This statement is not made to play down the significance of the other strokes or to diminish the importance of trying to master each and every stroke in order to become a complete, accomplished player.

Mastering the mechanics of the forehand alone will by no means guarantee success. The forehand, however, should be considered as the basic building block around which a total paddle game is constructed. Its fundamental importance is underscored by the fact that almost all successful top-flight tournament players and almost every accomplished club player I have ever seen have developed a good *consistent* and *offensive* forehand.

Theory: Let's briefly examine why the unique aspects of platform tennis as a game place such significance on the forehand.

The fundamental and distinctive characteristic of the game is that great equalizer, the *screening*. For paddlers the screens represent many things. The wires become a final line of defense, a form of reprieve if a player is overcommitted and out of position or overpowered. And, as we shall examine later, the screens can be used as an offensive weapon. The wires negate to a great extent the power hitter's bullet-like shots as well as the booming serve that dominates the opponent in other racquet games. The wires allow the receiver to play the ball softly and safely without being rushed. Thus a player can "cheat" by standing far to one side (the left side) when waiting to receive service and encourage a shot to his stronger forehand while protecting his backhand by offering a very small target to the server.

The server in paddle is allowed only *one serve;* therefore, the percentages of booming his delivery into the more open forehand area are very poor. Unlike tennis, where two serves are allowed, the platform tennis server cannot gamble with his serve. If a big serve is made, however, the receiver can allow the ball to rebound off the screening and more often than not he'll have an easy setup for a drive or lob return.

The relatively small size of the court and the speed with which the ball travels mean that a player does not have as much time to execute the mechanics of any one stroke as he does in, say, tennis. The extra split second of time available when making the forehand stroke (in contrast to the backhand) can sometimes mean the difference between returning or not returning a ball. Although I will describe stroke mechanics a little further on (and it should never be forgotten that all ground strokes should be hit out in front of you), it is possible, when you are hurried, to *gain* an invaluable *split second* with the *forehand.* The forehand is hit with the arm further from the ball when the body is positioned sideways to the oncoming ball; the backhand is hit with the arm closer to the ball. Thus an extra minisecond is gained on the forehand stroke.

Of immense importance to the use of the forehand in platform tennis is the almost too obvious and too easily taken for granted aspect of the game — your *partner!* Since platform tennis is a doubles game the mere physical presence of a partner on your side of the net immeasurably reduces the areas of open court available to your opponents. This fact enables you to take liberties when positioning yourself to protect your backhand and invite as many shots as possible to the forehand. Naturally your partner should be doing exactly the same. The elements of teamwork and covering for one another, therefore, become very important. Teamwork should not be underestimated by beginners or average players. The ability of partners to protect each other and to explore ways to achieve complete court coverage is not only a prerequisite for top competitive paddle but great fun and a satisfying aspect of the game at any level.

I have been very fortunate to have a partner whose extreme quickness and anticipatory skills are equaled only by his great competitive spirit. Bob Kingsbury's ability to chase down opponents' apparent winning shots and regain lost court position while still agilely covering for me is, in my opinion, almost without equal in paddle. The presence of such a partner enables me (or would enable anyone!) to take huge liberties in assuming the most advantageous court position for the execution of my forehand. The combination of two formidable forehands and a conscious effort to cover for each other makes a successful team and is a rewarding, enjoyable experience at any level of play. The importance of emphasizing teamwork, therefore, is even greater in platform tennis than in tennis because of the unique second-opportunity element in the game and the various levelers inherent in the sport.

Possibly the most important factor in understanding the vitalness of the forehand is its use as an offensive weapon. The return of service offers one of the few opportunities to hit out offensively and with real power. Even a very accomplished server in paddle can only hit the ball with about 50 percent of the speed of a normal hard tennis serve. This fact, coupled with the high bounce of the served ball, enables the receiver to step in and really hit down on the ball. Thus an interesting contrast to tennis develops in which the *receiver* can sometimes overwhelm the *server!* The control of the net, therefore, is vital when your team has the serve. Platform tennis is a doubles game and by effective utilization of a partner at the net the serving team can still retain a slight edge over the receiving team and more often than not will hold (win) the serve. The *offensive return,* however, is one way to overcome the serving team's advantage. Naturally if the forehand return is successfully put back in play but is weak and ineffectual, the serving team's chances of winning the point increase. The longer the serving team commands the net position the better its odds of winning the point. Simply put, the offensive forehand return is the surest and best percentage shot a receiving team will most likely have within a given rally to either win the point outright or to take away command of the net position from the serving team. An offensive forehand should be hit through your opponents. This will force them to retreat to play your ball off their screen, thus enabling your team to assume the dominant court position at net.

Another offensive opportunity will arise during a fast exchange of shots within a given point. The team that is not at net must be patiently and constantly looking for the moment to attack with a *forcing forehand drive*. This occurs when the level of the bouncing ball is high and provides a clear and unmistakable down angle for the hitter. You can also be aggressive with a rebounding *wire shot,* almost always the back wire (which will be described later).

All generalizations are dangerous, for there are always exceptions to prove them wrong. There are a number of good players with strong backhands, but they constitute a very small percentage, and their effectiveness comes more from the element of surprise than from consistency and/or a powerful stroke. The unique nature of platform tennis and its particular and peculiar demands place a far greater degree of importance on mastering a powerful, forcing forehand.

Mechanics: The fundamentals of actually executing a platform tennis forehand are few and very simple. As the stroke is technically easy to learn, most players try to do too much with the forehand, or they get

The standard forehand or Eastern grip. The paddle face is at right angles to the playing deck, and a player merely "shakes hands" with the handle to get the proper grip.

lazy in executing the basic mechanics. If there is a secret to a good forehand, it is simply to learn the fundamentals well and concentrate on exhaustive repetition of these precepts. Easier said than done!

The basic *Eastern* grip is the best. It is the most comfortable, switches quickly and easily to a backhand grip when necessary, is most convenient for striking high and low balls alike, and offers the accomplished player the most options for a variety of shots through slight movements of the wrist. The Eastern grip easily permits hitting the ball with a topspin that the more open Continental grip (toward the backhand) does not. The closed Western grip works effectively only on very high bouncing balls. In addition, these latter two grips limit the various options and shots available to the hitter.

For the correct Eastern grip simply "shake hands" with the paddle handle with the face of the paddle at a right angle to the deck. Make sure that the natural V formed by the spread between the thumb and fingers runs straight down the flat part of the handle. Some players recommend a slight spreading of the index finger for better "feel" and control. I do not. Keep the fingers together for a surer, firmer grip. Never change the basic grip and always be sure to relax your otherwise tight grasp on the handle between shots to avoid tiring the hand and forearm. Unlike tennis, squash, or badminton, platform tennis is played with a "dead" paddle; that is, there are no strings on the hitting surface with which to easily impart topspin or slice to the ball. A paddle forces the hitter to do all the work alone.

When receiving a serve or anticipating an opponent's shot your body should be in the ready position facing the net. Be relaxed yet on your toes in a comfortable, poised position with knees slightly bent and your weight leaning somewhat forward. You should use your other hand to loosely cradle the throat of your paddle in front of you. At the instant you determine a forehand ground stroke is the best shot for the approaching ball, turn your body sideways to the ball, paddle held back and high, weight on the back foot. The similarity between a baseball hitter's stance and swing and a paddle player's ground stroke is almost identical. The backswing is slightly shorter than in tennis because time and distance do not allow for a long backswing and because the distance you have to hit the ball is about one-half what it is in tennis. Some degree of backswing, however, is required for control and balance.

As you swing into the ball the most critical factor in a successful stroke occurs — your weight transfers from the back foot to the front at the same time as your hitting arm comes through. At the moment of impact, therefore, the entire force of your body weight moving forward is actually providing the power and ultimately the control for your arm and paddle. Your speed and control should not come from the arm or wrist but from body-weight transfer. This movement is not a stationary weight transfer. It is accomplished by stepping forward and into the line of the approaching ball with your front foot in coordinated timing with your striking arm and weight transfer. Impact should be made out in front of the body, which, in turn, helps you to hit off your front foot. You must "lean into" or "step into" the ball.

In a straight forehand return, your arm from backswing to impact moves across the center of your body and nearly parallel to the playing deck. By hitting up from under the ball and rolling your hitting forearm, you are applying topspin to the ball. Hitting up from under the ball is achieved by a slight rotation of the forearm and wrist to a degree that feels comfortable to each individual. The movement of the wrist comes before impact in order to enable your paddle to be under the ball as your paddle comes through and makes contact. Do not confuse a topspin return with being "wristy."

You must hit the ball with a firm, locked wrist, allowing the motion of your forearm to roll over at the moment of impact in order to give desired topspin to the ball. Speed and accuracy can only be attained with the application of topspin. The more you learn to exaggerate topspin, the more forceful you can become. Having made impact with the ball you must follow through for a controlled topspin drive. Without the followthrough, the above fundamental parts of the forehand stroke will be wasted.

Because of the relative closeness of your opponents and the speed at which the ball can travel, it is sometimes impossible to position your body and feet sideways in the prescribed manner. You are frequently required to make your shots from awkward, off-balance positions. In such instances a full and complete rotation of your hips and upper torso, especially the shoulders, will suffice to provide adequate body positioning and the underpinning necessary for an effective forehand. When hitting your forehand off balance be sure to take something off the ball and try a controlled, evenly paced shot rather than an overpowering one.

Taking a high, bounding screen shot that has rebounded far enough from the screen and toward the net at a sufficient height provides an excellent opportunity to drive offensively at your opponents, and you should not feel timid about doing it! The key is in determining whether the ball is high enough to afford a definite down angle into the opponents' court and at the same time allow the hitter to position himself comfortably and solidly in time to drive through the ball. When this golden opportunity occurs, you must hit the ball in front of your body, even though the ball, in this particular instance, is moving away from you and toward the net. For a split second you should actually be flowing toward the net with the rebounding ball as you "step into" the shot and drive through it with a topspin motion.

As the court is small the geometrical problem of driving a hard forehand up over the net and yet down into your opponents' court is a considerable challenge. Only with the application of topspin can a platform tennis player stroke the ball forcefully and have any chance for both accuracy and consistency.

Topspin provides the safety factor necessary for a hard-hit drive, as the ball spins in the direction of your opponent. This forward spinning action actually forces the ball's flight in a downward direction. A topspin return creates three problems for the opposition: it is a forcing drive with a certain degree of safety, it is difficult to volley against for the topspin when striking your opponent's paddle tends to spin off it in a downward direction, and it will skid slightly off the playing surface toward your opponent, thereby making the timing of his return more difficult.

Think positively as you are winding up to hit your forcing forehand. Don't try to "crush" every forehand, but be bold when the opportunity presents itself. If given a clear choice between lobbing or driving, and the odds of doing either successfully are about equal, you should hit the topspin forehand. Chances are in your favor that a properly executed, forceful shot will provide you and your partner with the offensive edge. Again, don't try to clobber every ball, but being able to produce an intimidating forehand with a high degree of consistency can be an awesome weapon in your platform tennis arsenal.

Herbert S. FitzGibbon II is a Princeton graduate and former nationally ranked tennis player who took up paddle a mere five years ago when his good friend John Beck first introduced him to the game. They began playing together and steadily improved their game. During the 1973–1974 winter season their practice and persistence in developing a unique style was perfectly suited for them and really paid off. They won every tournament in which they competed! Then they won "The Big One" — the U.S. Men's Doubles Championship in a stirring five-set victory. Herb is probably the "Dean" of the "New Breed." Combining lightning-fast reflexes with natural racquet ability, he has developed an all-around game. At thirty, Herb is destined to be a great player and champion for many years to come.

5. | HERBERT S. FITZGIBBON II

The Service

AFTER PLAYING in my first platform tennis tournament, I was most impressed (or perhaps I mean depressed!) by the difficulty I had effectively returning the services of a highly regarded team. I was also frustrated by the frequency with which my own service was slapped down at my feet or off the chest of my partner. The lesson I walked off the court with was that the service is the pivotal stroke of platform tennis. The serve is not as flashy or as much fun as a spectacular save in the deep corners or as awesome as a big forehand hit off the back wires, but it has the value that rebounding in basketball and interior blocking in football have. The team that serves consistently better than its opponents will usually win. Although not as devastating a weapon as in tennis, the paddle service is, indeed, the "bread and butter" stroke of the better platform tennis teams.

It is quite difficult to give a detailed description of how I serve in just one chapter. In addition, what I think I am doing may not appear at all that way to the observer. For these reasons, the *psychology* and *strategy* of serving will be emphasized, although some mention will be made of *technique*.

To discuss psychology before the ingredients of the actual service stroke may appear to be putting the cart before the horse, but I can think of two leading players in the game today who seem to prove Norman Vincent Peale's philosophy on the power of positive thinking.

The backhand or Continental grip is usually employed for the serve. The paddle face is more open than in a forehand grip, and the index finger is slightly separated from the others.

One of them is over forty, wears a back brace *and* a knee brace, and has the service motion of a pretzel. Despite these apparent handicaps, however, the last time he lost his service was just about two years ago on his opponent's lucky let cord winner (a ball that hits the top of the net and drops over into the opponent's court) in a friendly mixed doubles match! The other player is in his late twenties, a superb, natural athlete possessing a near perfect and powerful service action. He has discovered, much to his chagrin, that he can only serve overhand with confidence in practice or when he is way ahead or way behind. Under the pressure of competitive play, his service disintegrates.

The psychological problems for the serving paddler seem to arise principally from the fact that there is no second chance as there is in tennis. The luxury of the second service does not exist. Also, the tennis player is not obliged to follow his "cream puff" service to the net. In fact, if the tennis player is really having a difficult time serving, his partner can be brought back to the baseline to better defend himself. In paddle, however, there is no second opportunity, and, even worse, *the server must maintain and sustain the offensive by going in to the net behind his delivery or abandon all hope of winning.* The mental conflict is simple: do I hit the service hard and run the risk of faulting or do I "bloop" it in, charge the net, and pray the receiver will err?

During my first year of competitive platform tennis I hit the service perfectly flat, soft, and, on all but the "key" points, rather well placed. As I improved and began to play better opposition, however, it quickly became clear that a completely flat serve, unless exactly placed, could be attacked with regularity. When the big points came up, I found it almost impossible to hit the corners of the opponents' service box. I finally came to the conclusion that to serve a flat, soft ball to a good player was tantamount to faulting. I might get away with such a serve for one or two games, but over the period of a match the better players will eventually pounce on and demolish such a delivery.

After my initiation year in paddle I began to serve successfully because I came to realize that the service must be hit hard enough to allow my partner and me to maintain the offensive. Today I never think twice about hitting a big service on a crucial point, or about faulting, because the conflict has been resolved. The service is the most critical and vulnerable time for the offensive team, and if it is not executed in an offensive manner the initiative will pass from the server to the receiver. This attitude is all part of playing to win as against playing not to lose. There is a difference!

Once I had determined my service was to be a weapon and not merely a device for putting the ball into play, I actually developed it into a consistent, effective stroke. I used a modified tennis approach — and only, of course, after a great deal of practice! I hold the paddle for the service as I do in tennis — with a Continental grip. This in-between grip (between the forehand and backhand) allows me to apply plenty of spin (control) to the ball while still hitting with pace. Those players more comfortable with a flatter service will prefer a more closed or forehand grip, while others who hit with an exaggerated slice or twist will lean toward a backhand grip.

The toss-up is made with the arm completely outstretched with the ball being thrown forward and high enough to allow the hitting

A.

B.

A. At the start of the serve, weight is on the forward foot and the feet
   are set comfortably apart.

B. As paddle and ball come downward together, the weight should be
   shifted to the back foot.

C.

D.

C. Toss the ball forward. The front foot must not touch the base line
   until the ball has been hit.

D. Notice how far back paddle head is just prior to moving up and into
   the ball. Forward momentum and angle of body help the server to move
   quickly toward the net after he has served.

E.

F.

E. At the moment of impact, the server's arm is fully extended, and he begins to cross his back foot over the base line.

F. The server's followthrough is first out or forward, then down completely to his left side. He's now on his way to charging the net.

arm to be fully extended upon contact (thereby gaining maximum height). With my platform tennis toss-up the ball is lower and further in front of me than in my tennis toss because I really don't have to get my entire body weight into the serve. There is just not that much emphasis on power. If I time the ball well, the wrist snap, arm swing, and forward momentum of my body provide me with more than enough pace. Also, with a lower toss-up the full tennis serving motion would be very awkward and rushed. Granted, a higher toss-up would allow a full wind-up, but with such a small paddle and the relatively small service box, the bigger the motion the less control and the greater the number of variables and problems.

Instructors in every racquet and ball sport always stress "keep your eyes on the ball!" This is the rule I concentrate on most when I am serving. Once I am comfortably set and have determined where I am going to hit the ball, I then concentrate on a particular *spot* on the ball I want to strike. If I desire more spin, I look directly at the *top* of the ball and that is where I aim to make contact. To apply less spin and attain more speed, I make contact with the right side of the ball. In neither case do I stop looking at the ball until *after* I have hit it. Such unwavering concentration combined with keeping my *head up* for as long as possible reduces the chances of faulting into the net.

An important element in my service is the "feeling of *flowing*" in toward the net as I contact the ball. By flowing rather than recklessly running toward the net I do not hurry the swing in my haste to rush in as far as possible. My forward momentum plus two quick steps allows me to volley confidently and comfortably all but the shortest, softest, and lowest returns and at a level above my knees. Handling the really short, soft returns is my partner's responsibility. I try to serve hard enough so that he does not have to be back on his heels. He is in a perfect volleying position only if he is confident that he is not going to get creamed because of a "fat, hanging" service. If he has to "defend himself at all times," he won't be any help to me and will probably be a hindrance because of his understandable tentativeness.

So far I have tried to convey the proper psychological attitude for effective, consistent serving — hit the service hard enough to maintain the offensive — and my technique for the delivery — a modified, contained tennis swing and motion with plenty of spin applied to the ball. One final ingredient remains — the *strategy* of serving.

I consider *spin* and ball placement to be far more important than speed. (Naturally a combination of all three is ideal!) A well-placed, flat service can be timed easily by the receiver, but it also presents control problems for the server. A spinning ball, on the other hand, tends to vary from serve to serve, even though I think I am hitting it the same way. The spin prevents the receiver from timing his returns. Spin throws off his rhythm and is a more difficult shot to control. Spin, however, aids my control. When I step up to the base line to start my delivery I decide which part of the opponents' service box I will try to hit to. Then I pick a spot approximately *three feet* above the height of the net, toss up the ball, and concentrate on watching it until I have hit that imaginary three-foot mark with heavy spin. As long as I keep my head up and don't ease up on my swing, the service has plenty of spin and speed and almost never goes into the net. Really what I am doing is spot bowling. The three-foot spot prevents the spin from dipping into the net and also keeps the ball from going long.

In the forehand court I try to place almost 90 percent of my serves down the center toward the (right-hand opponent's) backhand. If an opponent can run around my service to hit a forehand and still not expose the entire side of his court, then I vary my serving by occasionally hitting wide to his forehand corner. In the backhand (ad) court it is much more difficult to force an opponent to hit a backhand. While I try to move the ball around to keep the receiver off balance, I do not strain needlessly and endlessly to hit to the deep, backhand corner. About the best I can hope for when serving into the ad court is to "jam" or crowd the receiver. Most players can run around any but the most perfectly placed serves and hit a forehand. If the service, however, is deep and hit with heavy spin, the offensive will still remain with you. The point I am trying to make here is that I will sacrifice corner placement for speed and spin if necessary. If I am experiencing difficulty in getting my service into the backhand court, I will eventually abandon the attempt and just hit quite hard down the center or directly at the receiver. Even though he may know where the ball is going, the speed and spin should prevent him from doing much with his return.

Unswerving confidence that you can hit a big service into your opponent's court consistently comes only from the experience of having done it time after time — and under the pressure of tournament play. The actual execution must occur before you gain this all-important confidence. A positive attitude, however, as mentioned previously, is an essential springboard toward ultimately developing an excellent service. Then, of course, as in anything, *practice* is an absolute necessity for the evolution of a consistent and effective service. One hour a weekend of serving will improve not only your delivery but your entire game by at least 20 percent. There is nothing more uplifting than really believing or, even better, *knowing* you will hold your service next time you are up.

Douglas Russell, a thirty-year-old "swinging" bachelor who recently turned in his stockbroker's pinstripes to become a tennis and paddle professional, had the dubious pleasure and arduous task of "carrying" Dick Squires during the 1971–1973 seasons. One of the most graceful backhand court-side stylists in the game, Doug owns all the "classic" platform tennis shots. He is one of the few top performers who can confidently "whip" an offensive backhand return off the back or back and side screening. Doug has a tantalizing touch and one of the most consistent and damaging topspin forehand returns.

6. | DOUGLAS RUSSELL

Return of Service

THE RETURN OF SERVICE may be the most important offensive shot in platform tennis. It is impossible to win a set on your service alone. You must break the opponents' service at least once, and to do this you must have a winning return of service.

A receiver in platform tennis has an advantage over other racquet sports players in that the opposing server is allowed only one delivery. He cannot blithely blast the "cannon ball" and feel secure in the knowledge that if he faults, he still has another chance. The single service in paddle is an intriguing discipline — and also character building! The receiver has another advantage. If a service gets by him, he can still play the ball "off the wires."

The fundamentals of a good return of service are

1. Concentration
2. Anticipation
3. Court positioning — where to stand
4. Body positioning — how to stand
5. Ability
6. Attitude
7. Practice

Let's review each of these elements in some detail.

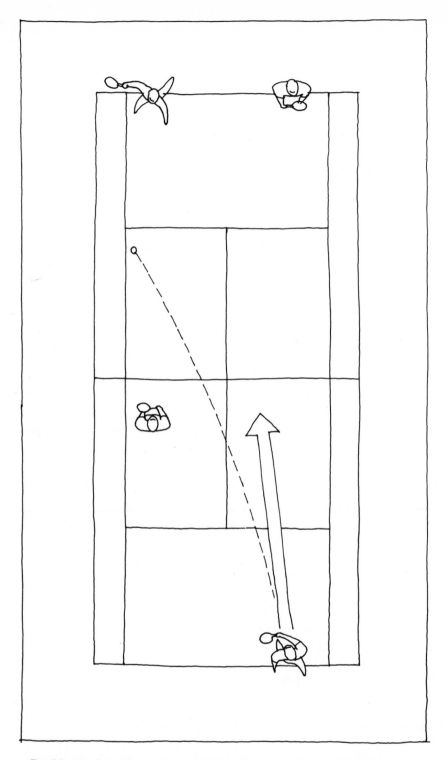

Doubles tactics: The server must *always* go to the net behind his serve.
Both teammates on the receiving team should be back at the base line.
The basic rule of thumb in platform tennis doubles is that partners
should be either up at the net together or back at the base line together.

Concentration

You must block out the surroundings, the noises, the distractions, your aches and pains, even thoughts about your luscious date after the match, or the previous shot you just "blew" at a crucial point. You must think only of the upcoming service. The more effective tournament players seem to be wearing earmuffs and blinders. They are oblivious to sights and sounds as they await the opponent's delivery.

Anticipation

You must consciously try to outthink the server — to anticipate where and how the service will land in your service box. Where is the server standing? If he is near the center serving line, he can serve easily down the center and it is more difficult for him to hit a sharply angled service. On the other hand, if he is standing wide of the center line, his service must travel at an angle across the court. How does he serve? Is his service always the same? A flat service? A spin service? Or a combination of both types? Does he consistently serve to the same spot in the receiving court, or does he move the ball around? And does he tend to ease up on the important points?

Your analysis and answers to these questions can be extremely significant when determining just where and how you will position yourself to receive the service. Some of these questions can be answered during the warm-up. Other answers will become apparent only as the game progresses. But learning the answers as soon as possible will give you, the receiver, a definite edge in handling the return of service, as well as in anticipating where to best position yourself.

Court positioning

In most instances you should stand on or just inside the baseline so that you can hit a return of service waist high as the ball rises. If the services frequently land short, stand further forward. But remember, it is always easier and wiser to be moving forward when hitting the ball than to be retreating.

Chances are you can make a more effective return of service off your forehand, so position yourself toward the backhand side of the court in order to open up the service box to your forehand.

Body positioning

Stand facing the server in the "ready position" — knees slightly bent, feet comfortably apart, in a slight forward crouch, with the weight on the balls of your feet. Hold your paddle with a forehand grip, slightly above the waist and angled toward the server. In this position you are ready to spring, to move forward toward the net, to attack, to handle almost any service effortlessly and effectively.

Ability

By "ability" I mean hand-eye coordination, reflexes, speed, fine footwork, and consistency. Natural athletes are blessed with innate ability along these lines. But anyone can take steps to improve his overall performance in these important areas. For example, I have found table tennis to be very helpful in quickening both my hand-eye coordination and my reflexes. I often play table tennis the night before an important platform tennis tournament. Speed can be increased by jogging for conditioning and wind sprints for acceleration. Consistency can be improved by practicing percentage shots.

Attitude

Execute your return of service with an "I can win" point of view. Positive and aggressive thinking can be extremely helpful. First and foremost, the ball must be returned! Second, keep the ball low. It may catch the server at his feet before he has reached the net. Even if he has attained a position at the net, he will be forced to hit up to you or to strike the ball so close to the net that he cannot make a powerful shot. Third, be aggressive. Hit with controlled power. The ball is heavy, the paddle is heavy, so don't merely push the ball. Hit it!

Practice

Practice is of paramount importance in any sport. It is not enough, however, to just hit with somebody or even to practice by playing. The service return should be practiced as a separate entity. This is something that can be done best with one other player. Find a friend who wants to practice his service. Twenty or thirty minutes of returning serves should do wonders for both his and your service returns. Practice several times a month and you will really sharpen (and expand) your repertoire of returns. Practice of service returns is very important. On a forehand or backhand serve deep in the court you must often shorten the backswing because a fast service will not give you the time for a full stroke. The best way to develop your own quick response to a hard, deep serve is to practice returning such serves.

Types of service returns are

1. Forehand drive (topspin, flat)
2. Backhand
3. Dink
4. Lob
5. Return off the wires (defensive, offensive)
6. Blitzing

Forehand drive

The forehand return is both the most frequent and most desirable shot to hit. There are two basic forehand drives — topspin and flat. The topspin forehand return of service is preferable because it can clear the net with some margin of error and still drop into the court. A hard-hit flat drive, on the other hand, must be executed almost perfectly to keep the ball from going into the net or sailing out past the baseline.

The forehand return is the most powerful service return. The topspin forehand is the shot I prefer to make on nearly all my returns. I position myself for it. I practice it. It is by far the most aggressive return of service. The topspin forehand can produce winning returns and often force errors by opponents.

I return all services holding the paddle with a forehand grip. I hope the service will come to my forehand. Even if it does not, I don't feel I have time to change the grip, so I use the conventional Eastern forehand grip for all my service returns.

The majority of the forehand service returns should be hit across the center of the net where the net is at its lowest point. In addition, the ball is headed cross court at an angle toward the far back corner, which gives the shot the greatest length of the court. An occasional return should be hit down the line or directly at the opposing net man. This tactic accomplishes two things: it tests the reflexes of the net man and also keeps him from poaching.

Backhand

Despite the fact that you have positioned yourself to make a forehand return, a skillful server may still be able to direct a service to your backhand. As you are in position for a forehand and are holding the paddle in a forehand grip, a backhand return can be a difficult shot. An effective topspin backhand is very hard to hit and control. The best percentage shot, therefore, is to slice the ball low over the net between your two opponents. Again, an occasional backhand hit either down the line or directly at the opposing net man to keep him off balance is desirable.

Dink

A dink is a blocked return of service with little power and with a slight amount of applied backspin that crosses close to the top of the net. It will drop to the playing surface close to the net if not volleyed by your opponents. It can be effectively hit on either the forehand or backhand sides. A dink is like a baseball pitcher's "change-up" — it serves as a change of pace to throw off your opponents' rhythm. It should never be hit to the opposing net man because he can usually return it quite easily.

The dink is most effective when hit across the center of the net. This is the shortest distance for it to travel and places the ball between your two opponents. An alternative is a sharply angled cross-court dink that falls just over the net and just inside the outer sidelines of the

Doug Russell executes a "dink" backhand return of serve. Notice that
he is moving in on the ball, and he will not move the paddle too
far forward on his followthrough as he is hitting a short, sharply angled,
delicate shot.

court. This shot is harder to execute successfully since the net is higher at this point and there is the chance that the ball will drop wide of the court. In addition, since this shot must travel further, the advancing server has more time to reach it. The cross-court dink is also easier for your opponents since there is no confusion about who should hit it — as there frequently is on balls placed down the center of the court.

Lob

The lob is basically a defensive return and is used in championship platform tennis when it is difficult to make an offensive return. The lob is certainly the easiest return to make. There is no possibility of netting the ball, which should be hit several feet inside the baseline. A perfect lob — which drops just inside the opposition's baseline — is rarely a winner. Don't attempt this shot often because it can very easily go out for a lost point and is not very difficult for opponents to return.

I often use the lob return when a hard spin serve is hit high and deep to my backhand. I also lob occasionally for a change of pace to break up my competition's rhythm and to throw off their anticipation. If it's a sunny day, I lob when my opponents will have to look up into the sun to hit the ball. The lob return can also result in an occasional winner, especially if the server is charging the net like an irate elephant. The key to an effective lob is "holding" your shot until the very last second. The opponents will be leaning forward anticipating a drive. If your lob does clear your adversaries' outstretched paddles and lands in the court, be sure to take advantage of your shot by quickly moving in toward the net. In other words, the lob return can also be an offensive weapon.

Return off the Wires

Service returns off the wires are usually defensive and are often desperation shots. Frequently the receiver has very little maneuvering room. Also, if the ball has hit the side screen as well as the back screen, it can be traveling at an unusual angle. For these reasons, a service return off the wires should almost always be lobbed. Occasionally, however, a service that comes both straight and high off the back wires can be driven aggressively. This can be a highly effective service return, but it takes perfect timing to achieve and therefore should only be attempted by the more advanced players. A hard drive is the most difficult of all aggressive service returns off the screening.

Blitzing

Blitzing is following the return of service to the net in order to be in a position to volley the next shot past your opponents. Blitzing, although dangerous, is often effective because it is so unnerving to your opponents. As the servers, they customarily command the net. An effective blitz either results in an outright winner for you or a situation in which you have appropriated the net position from the serving team. Blitzing, however, requires a good return of service, quick reflexes, boldness, and a partner who stays back at the center of the baseline and covers your court if the ball is volleyed past you.

The best time to blitz is when receiving a short, high service. Your own return can be either a drive or a dink. The important thing is to hit a shot that your opponents must hit up to you — in other words, your return must be low. You should be moving in aggressively, ready to volley the ball up the center of the court between your opponents or right at them.

It is easier to blitz from the backhand or ad court than from the forehand or deuce court. This is because as you approach the net most shots will be coming to your forehand, which (for most players) is an easier shot to volley. The backhand court player also is given a much wider angle to shoot for.

Ten "Musts" to Improve Your Return of Service
1. Concentrate
2. Anticipate
3. Practice
4. Set yourself comfortably and be ready when opponent serves
5. Get paddle back quickly
6. Move in on ball catching it on the rise
7. Return forehand across center of net
8. Lob occasionally
9. Blitz if possible
10. Change for pace effectiveness

Edward L. Winpenny, Jr., one of the most exciting players in
the history of the game, was a National Mixed Doubles champion in
1958 (with Louise Raymond) and National Men's Doubles champion
in 1966 (with Dick Squires). He was also "bridesmaid" in the Mixed
in 1961 and ran second in the Men's in 1961, 1962, and 1965. In 1953,
the first tournament in which he competed, Ted and his partner Bill
Cooper reached the semifinals of the National Men's Doubles, and he
accomplished the same feat sixteen years later with partner John
Mangan. Over the years Ted has climbed many miles of screening in
the process of returning opponents' shots. He claims that his greatest
thrill was winning the 1966 U.S. Men's Doubles, losing only twenty-one
games in fifteen sets of top-flight competition. An intense, colorful
competitor, Ted had an innate sense of the opposition's weaknesses
and exploited them unmercifully. A stockbroker, residing in New
Canaan, Connecticut, Ted spends much of his time in local politics,
fishing, and playing weekend paddle — just for fun.

7. | EDWARD L. WINPENNY, JR.

The Volley

THE VOLLEY is definitely one of the most important strokes in the game of paddle. Most of the better players in tennis and platform tennis alike will tell you the game is won or lost by controlling the net. Overheads and volleys, therefore, are of paramount importance.

Keep in mind that the screening completely surrounding the playing surface of the court — off which you can make returns (a dimension not present in tennis) — calls for a different game strategy. Unlike most racquet games you are confronted with the somewhat frustrating (also intriguing) inability to hit an outright winner by sheer power and strength. This unique ingredient also increases the enjoyment of the game by prolonging the rallies, balancing the games, and equalizing the abilities of the less physically endowed when up against the overpowering strong-armed types.

The volley, as in tennis, has the same basic objectives — to control the net and ultimately to win the point with a well-aimed placement. Also the types of volleys (to be discussed later) have the same general names and are basically executed with a tennis motion. Because of the paddle, the size of the court, and the weight of the ball, however, the differences in strategy, court positioning, and stroke production between platform tennis and tennis are quite obvious and axiomatic.

The wooden hitting surface of the paddle obviously does not offer much resiliency and the success of the stroke depends on the player's

Dick Squires in the "ready" position at the net. Note the wide stance and slightly bent knees, which will help him move quickly in either direction. The paddle is held in front with the paddle head up. He studies his opponent for a clue that will enable him to anticipate the return. His grip on all volleys is toward the backhand.

ability to hit the ball in the center of the paddle. He will not have the helpful "whip" the tennis player has when meeting the ball with a tightly strung racquet. Because of this factor, the first thing you must understand is that the proper position for volleying is *in close* to the net — no further away than three to four feet. Next you must grip the paddle very *tightly* and maintain an extra-firm wrist at the point of contact since the entire impact must be absorbed by your arm. The platform tennis ball is heavier and denser than a tennis ball, and your paddle should not turn in your hand or "give" when you are executing a stiff, crisp volley.

Because of the relative smallness of the court, a player at the net will have much less time between the stroke of his opponent and his volley return. The "ready position" at the net, therefore, dictates a slightly different grip and court position than you employ for tennis. In tennis the net player normally holds his racquet up and at right angles to the net. In paddle, however, it is much wiser to hold the paddle somewhat parallel to the net — as if prepared for a *backhand* volley. As the distance between opponents becomes smaller the time to change from a backhand to a forehand position is lessened. A more accomplished platform tennis player therefore tends to hit more than half of his volleys from the backhand stance and side. Because of the lack of time, it is best to become accustomed to employing only one grip for all your volleying — a grip that is slightly open and toward the backhand grip.

There are many different types of volleys — drop, stop, half, approach, forcing, lob, return of service, etc. My comments will be generally confined to those volleys and other net play shots in which the stroke, the thought, and the purpose (strategy) behind the stroke are important.

When one team has attained control of the net in any given rally it has seemed energy-conserving to me for the backhand partner to position himself a foot or so further back from the net than his forehand teammate. In this position it is not necessary for both partners to be constantly going back for lobs, which will be more effortlessly handled by the backhand court player. Next time you are watching top-flight tournament players, note that the backhand side partner invariably takes the bulk of the overhead returns — which are truly easier for him to return. At the same time, the forehand court partner (to cut across the court and intercept his partner's shot) should be ready at every moment and at the opportune time to "poach" and volley a soft return hit in the direction of his backhand player. When this occurs, of couse, the two teammates reverse positions.

Half volleys are a frequently used stroke for the aggressive and more accomplished tennis player. In platform tennis, however, it never has been as useful a stroke primarily because of the small size of the court. If you are forced to half-volley a soft shot you may well find yourself way out of position when the opponents volley directly back at your feet. Also, if you try to half-volley a hard-hit ball that lands fairly deep toward your base line you will quickly learn the percentages are better to let the ball bounce and then return it as it rebounds off the screen. By allowing the ball to go into the back wires you will be given more time to execute the proper return. Also, a more aggressive shot might be made because of your patience and self-discipline.

When viewing a typical paddle match you will note that the more inexperienced player will make one error after another when hitting his first volley on the dead run as he approaches the net after his serve. The main reason for his persistent erring is that he is not making contact with the ball with his *feet planted* firmly on the deck. The more accomplished player will not be running full-tilt when he makes impact with the ball. In order to make a proper return-of-service volley the server should make his approach to the net in two steps — approximately two thirds of the way in on what Allison Danzig once described as a "volatile volleying venture" — in which he anchors himself and makes a sure-footed volley and then moves up to a more normal net position; i.e., closer to the net. Volleys hit on the run are invariably hard to control and have a tendency to "fly long" because of the momentum behind them.

One of the key shots in the net game repertoire is the approach volley made after a good return of service. In tennis the partner of the player returning service normally assumes a position close to the net (just inside the service line), hoping that if his partner's return is a good one he will be able to poach and put away the server's return. This is not sound strategy in platform tennis!

Again, because of the smallness of the court the serving team will

Dick Squires hits the vital return of service volley. He will move further
toward the net after successfully blocking this shot deep to the
opponents' backcourt. Notice his arm is fully extended, and contact with
the ball is made well in front of his body. His feet are positioned
sideways to the net and are firmly anchored to the court before
he hits the volley.

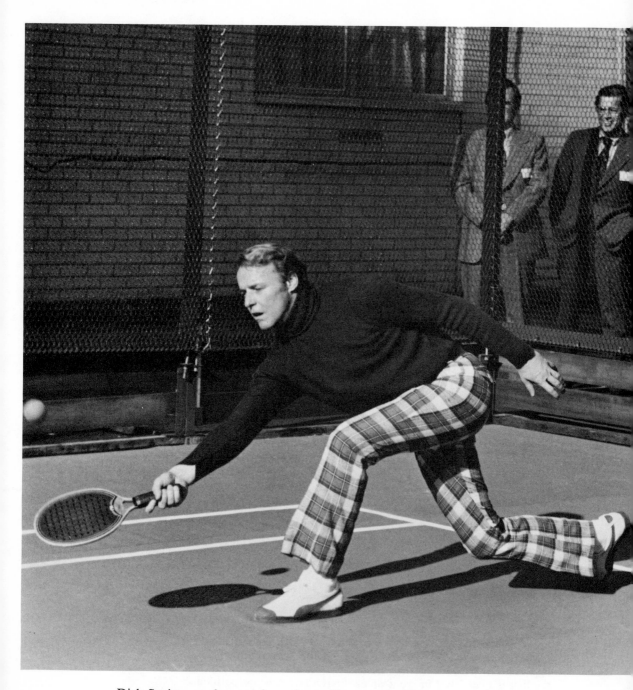

Dick Squires reaches out for a low volley return. He uses extended index finger for more "feel" on all his volleys. His paddle face is open to help project the ball over the net.

usually assume its positions at the net in a shorter time span than in tennis. If the player returning the serve hits a feeble shot the offensive team will volley right through the defenseless partner if he is at the net. So the rule of thumb in platform tennis is that the teammates receiving the serve should stay back together near the baseline. You just cannot play one up and one back because of the short distance between you and the opposition.

There is one exception to this rule, however, and it can only be performed successfully by more experienced players. This is the tactic of blitzing. If the player returning service feels he has made a shot that will force the in-coming server to return a volley from a low position near his sneakers, then he, and he alone, should follow his return to the net. If his assessment of the effectiveness of the stroke has been accurate he will, by himself, be able to attain the net and hit a winning volley through the opponents. Incidentally, this volley should be hit in such a manner that it will "die" as it reaches the side or corner wires. When the return of service is well stroked, the server's volley is frequently a "sitter" (an easy putaway), and the natural tendency is to kill it. Again, patience and experience will eventually prove to you that a sure, delicately placed volley will win the majority of points for your team. So the only time teammates are not up at net together or back at the base line together is during the act of blitzing and, of course, when lining up to serve. In this particular instance the blitzer's partner stays in the middle of the backcourt just in case his net-rushing teammate's return is not as effective as he had hoped.

Another important aspect of volleying is the "art" of poaching. Again, because the court is so narrow, there are innumerable opportunities to cross over, cut off the opposition's returns, and hit a drop volley (a deftly placed "touch shot" that just barely clears the net and dies) — particularly when your partner has made a good serve. The drop volley is especially effective when dropped on the side of the non-returner, because, as mentioned previously, the service returner's partner should remain in a deep court position in case his teammate attempts to gain the net behind his return.

When one reviews the various volleying techniques, then puts them into practice, he quickly discovers that, important as volleying is, so is knowing when *not* to hit a volley! When you and your partner have gained the offensive net position you can win points by making well-placed volleys and overheads (either down the middle between the opponents or deep toward the back corners), but you can also win many points by not hitting the ball! In the middle of a long, heated rally the tendency (when up at the net) is to hit anything you can reach. Time and experience will teach you there are two reasons to resist this temptation: first, a ball hit at shoulder height with reasonable pace will invariably be a point for your side if allowed to float over the base line, and second, if there is any doubt as to whether the ball will be in or out, there are three reasons to consider letting it go: (1) it may go out, which means you win the point, (2) if it lands in your court, you always have a good chance of retrieving it off the back screen, and (3) you have added an enticing element and quality to your net game. If you and your partner hit nearly *every* ball that comes your way at the net your opponents have no reason to be careful. They will feel they can hit harder and harder until eventually they will force you into an error. On the other hand, if you use discretion and let some of their balls go through, even though some may go in, they will have to change their game. They will become more cautious when they realize you are not going to hit everything within reach of your paddles.

You should strive to "spank" your volleys hard enough to land them *deep* in the opponent's court. Unless you are executing a drop volley, your net shots should bounce beyond the service lines. Depth will keep the opponents back and on the defensive.

The "perfect" volley is aimed deep in the opposition's backcourt and right at the *corners*. Ideally, if properly placed, the ball will be dying as it approaches the back screen. Another spot to aim for is deep and down the *center*. The open space between teammates has always been an area that is vulnerable. Unless the partners have played a great deal together there is frequently hesitation and uncertainty as to which one will handle the return. Sometimes both go for it, other times neither — in both cases you have made a volleying winner! The other rule of thumb pertaining to volleying placement is to aim right *at the feet* of your opponents — especially if one of them is beginning to move inside the base line or if you have drawn him in on your previous shot and he is attempting to scramble back. Aim for his sneakers!

Finally, try to place all your volleys with a *purpose*. Obviously the best placement and strategy is "hitting 'em where they ain't." Since the court is small and relatively easy to cover, it might take several shots before you accomplish a winner or a forced error. Remember, in this marvelous racquet game more than any other, patience is a virtue!

David R. Jennings, 40 years old, was twice a member of a National Championship team. In 1964 and 1967 he and Oliver Kimberly won the U.S. Men's Doubles title. For five consecutive years (1960–1965), they dominated the field in the important Connecticut State tournament, and they've also taken home trophies from the Buffalo, Short Hills, and Rye Invitationals. Known for his famous black English derby, which miraculously never seems to fall off his head even during the most heated rallies, Dave aptly sums up his feelings about paddle: "No racquet sport is easier to learn and enjoy so quickly. Truly a game for men and women of all age levels."

8. | DAVID R. JENNINGS

The Lob

To LOB, by definition, is to hit a ball high to the back of the opponents' court.

The game of platform tennis is characterized by three very unique features:

1. The court is only one quarter the size of a regular tennis court.
2. Only one serve is allowed.
3. A hard-hit ball that bounces deep within the playing area can be returned off the tensioned wires if the ball doesn't hit the deck a second time (screen play).

All three of these distinctive features negate the power type of game associated with tennis. The strategy is, therefore, to keep the ball in play and wait for your opponents to make an error or provide you with an opportunity to hit a forcing shot that causes an error or perhaps even results in an outright winner.

The lob is probably the *most frequently hit shot* in platform tennis. There are basically two types of lobs — offensive and defensive. The majority of lobs will be executed for defensive purposes, but many of them will be hit with the intent of setting up the opposition in order to eventually take the offensive. Many platform tennis players consider the lob to be a "holding action" until the opponents make a mistake.

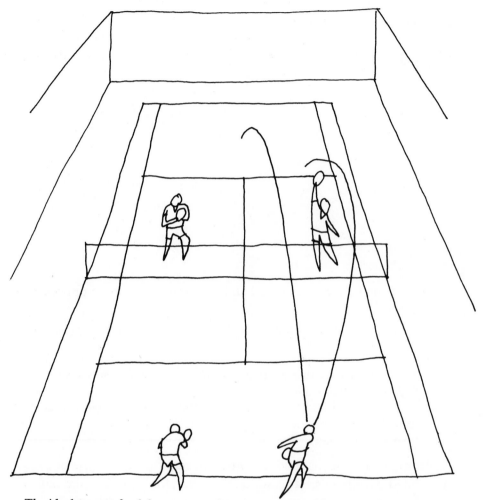

The ideal targets for lobs are over the opponents' backhands or down the middle of the court.

Once a person has generally mastered the art of playing the screens and feels confident that there are few shots he cannot retrieve off the wires, then platform tennis takes on it fullest dimensions and is most enjoyable. *It is in screen play where the lob is most often employed.*

The normal tendency of unknowing beginners — when playing balls off the screens — is to swing too fast with the paddle face at right angles to the deck. It is natural (but entirely wrong) to want to hit every shot hard — to try to end the point quickly with a sensational return. This tendency usually results in line drives into the net or over the opponents' base line. Novices try to do too much with the ball, and the end result is a "poor percentage" shot. It should be understood that the screens tend to slow down the momentum of the ball, thus allowing the player more time than might be expected. In other words, the screens afford the player both a second opportunity and the luxury of extra precious seconds to get into proper position when returning the ball. There is no reason to rush or panic. Slow down! You have a great deal more time than you think — so use it!

When your opponents have the advantage of being up at net and your team is back at the base line, your main objective is to try to force them back and gain control of the net position. The ideal lob would catch the opposition tight at the net, go over their heads and outstretched paddles, and bounce fairly deep in their back court — allowing you and your partner to move forward immediately and take control of the net. A lob placed over their heads and deep into their backcourt is a particularly good shot, because it forces the opponents to drop back from the net in order to hit an overhead. A well-placed deep lob puts pressure on the opponents to hit a deep overhead to your backcourt and opens up the possibility that they may hit the ball either into the net or out over the base line. Or they might hit a weak overhead just over the net, which allows you to move in and hit down on the ball. This shot could provide you with the opportunity to take control of the net or force your opponents to err.

As the ball is hit by your opponents (who are up at the net), instantly position yourself approximately two feet away from the back wires and close to where you believe the ball will bound into the screen. As the ball approaches get your paddle back, hold it firmly, and open the face to about a 45-degree angle to the deck. Let the ball go by you and hit into the screen. As it bounds out, make contact with your paddle *under* the ball and concentrate on hitting it both forward and up. Try to attain *both* height and depth with your lob. Follow through as you would for any other ground stroke; however, when lobbing, your followthrough will be slightly more upward and outward.

The placement of the lob should be toward your opponents' *backhand* side or down the *middle* between them to cause confusion or hesitation as to which player will return it. If the sun is a factor, try to lob to the opposing teammate who appears to be most bothered by it. This is not unsportsmanlike strategy, and you can be sure in competitive platform tennis your opponents will do the same to you when you change court sides!

As a general rule of thumb, you should, when returning certain balls, hit a lob off the screens when the ball is descending and is below your chest. Any other shot would be considered "poor percentage" and not conducive to keeping the ball in play.

The lob can also be employed effectively on the return of service. In today's more aggressive style of attacking the serve, a well-placed lob as a change of pace can catch the server rushing in to make a volley or the net man leaning toward the net too much. Analyze your opponents' moves to recognize just when a lob might be most effectively used as an offensive weapon. Should an unexpected well-placed serve catch you out of position, use the lob rather than try to crack a hard return while off balance. By lobbing you are keeping the ball in play instead of making a needless and probable error. Also remember that extremely hard hit serves may be played off the screens and a lob return, in this case, will keep you in the point.

Doing the unexpected keeps your opponents off balance and "edgy." Don't always hit the same shots in similar situations. The lob volley, for instance, can be a very offensive shot — especially when the opposition does not anticipate it. Imagine all four players at net volleying back and forth when suddenly the ball is arched over the opponents' heads when a hard volley was expected at their feet. This is a "touch" shot that takes much practice but can become a sure winner when used at just the right moment. The lob volley, is, however, probably the most difficult and dangerous of all strokes. It has to be perfectly executed to be successful. Anything short of perfection will undoubtedly result in your having to "eat the ball," since you are at net and precariously vulnerable.

To become an effective lobber you must practice hitting different types of lobs every time you play, developing your knowledge of the degree of paddle face angle best for each, how hard to hit the ball, how fast a swing is necessary, and the degree of height and length you wish to attain.

Because of all the unique equalizers in the game of platform tennis (smaller court, single serve, and the screen play) you need not be too fearful if you lob short and low. Unlike regular tennis — where such a lob is usually a setup for a winning shot by your opponent — a shallow lob in paddle is rarely fatal. There is no need to strive to hit every lob so that your ball lands on the base line. Again, there is no percentage in shooting for such perfection. As a matter of fact, such a seemingly ideal, deep lob is not as effective as one that lands just behind your opponent. The deeper the lob, the better the chances are that your opposition will be able to retrieve it off the back screening.

Everyone has basically the same strokes, but their degree of proficiency varies. The reason for this variation really boils down to how much a player wants to practice in order to develop his expertise. This is certainly true when developing an effective lob. How good you become in your lobbing is directly proportional to how much you practice — both in fun matches as well as under competitive playing conditions. Lobbing is not difficult, but to develop a consistent lob, and a variety of defensive and offensive lobs, does require time and effort.

Robert Kingsbury is John Mangan's "set 'em up" forehand court
player, and Bob and John dominated the platform tennis scene from
1970 until they were beaten in the quarter-finals of the 1974 Nationals.
In 1970, 1971, and 1972, they won the Connecticut State title. In 1971
and 1973, they were victorious in Cleveland and also took the Greenwich
Invitational in 1973. They were finalists in the 1970 and 1971
National Men's and finally won the coveted title in 1972 and 1973.
In addition, Bob and John annexed the First Annual Vat 69 Gold Cup
at Hilton Head, South Carolina, in November 1973 — winning the
title over the top fifteen-ranked teams in the country. An advertising
executive, Bob lives in Scarsdale, New York, the birthplace of platform
tennis. In 1974, he and wife Clare made the semifinals of the National
Mixed Doubles, then lost to his close friend and perennial partner,
John Mangan and Gloria Dillenbeck. Because of his aggressive play,
highly competitive spirit, and tremendous speed, Bob has been nicknamed
"The Road-runner of Platform Tennis." At thirty-eight, Bob is
considered to be as fine a forehand court player as any playing the game.

9. | ROBERT KINGSBURY

The Overhead

ONE OF THE cardinal sins in the game of platform tennis is erring on a simple overhead. May it never happen to you, but when it does — as it surely will — chances are you are trying to do too much with the shot.

Think along with me about a routine, long, steady point — the kind of rally you have played (or one day, as you improve, will play) a hundred times. Your partner has served, successfully gained control of the net with a good volley off the service return, and now the two of you are at the net — against opponents in the backcourt — engaged in the often exciting, sometimes dull, process of waiting for an opening. While you are waiting, your opponents are throwing up lobs, short and long, and you are returning their balls with overheads. The point will be decided when one of three things happens. The opponents may hit an exceptionally fine lob, forcing a very weak return off your overhead from which they can attack. End of point. Or, you can hit a winning overhead off a short lob — an overhead that is virtually unreturnable. Again, end of point. Or you can make an error in your overhead by hitting it into the net, wide or long. My hope in this chapter is to help you select and hit the right overhead at the right time *and* to help you avoid making errors at any time.

Let's get down to some fundamentals, the four "P's": position, pace, placement, and patience.

1. *Position* — I have always been a strong believer in the importance of body position for any shot in platform tennis. If your body is in the right spot, in proper balance and control, you are 90 percent on the way toward executing a good shot. This theory certainly applies to overheads.

If your opponent's lob is shallow, chances are you are standing in the right place to hit the overhead. All you need do is turn your body slightly sideways, as if you were about to serve, wait, then hit, moving into the ball with an abbreviated service motion and a standard service grip. I say "abbreviated" as usually you will only have time to start from the second half, or "cocked" phase of the normal service delivery motion. Always keep the ball out in front of you, and at the moment of impact extend your forearm fully in order to attain maximum height.

If the lob is deeper, your first and immediate move should be backward. Move quickly to a point beneath or just beyond the depth of the lob, set your feet, turn your body sideways, and proceed with the execution of your stroke. But *first,* get yourself set up in the right position.

2. *Pace* — Unlike tennis, power is not required when hitting an overhead in paddle. Rarely will you hit this particular shot with all the muscle you can muster. Rather, you will attempt to vary the pace of the overhead in order to match the purpose and placement of the shot. As a matter of fact, most of the more effective overhead shots I will be describing are hit so softly that anyone, old or young, male or female, can properly execute them. Anyone can hit a winner off the overhead using his or her brains — not brawn. The vast majority of paddle overheads are hit with *subtlety.* So relax! Forget about putting the ball away every time with overwhelming power and concentrate on placement.

3. *Placement* — Here is the *key* to the overhead. As I have said, it is not how hard you hit the ball but *where* you hit it that counts. There are several "target areas" on a platform tennis court that should be considered ideal spots to aim for when hitting your overheads.

First, there is the "safe" shot — the one you will be hitting most of the time. Against a team of two right-handers, the safe shot is down the middle, slightly left of center, favoring the backhand side of the

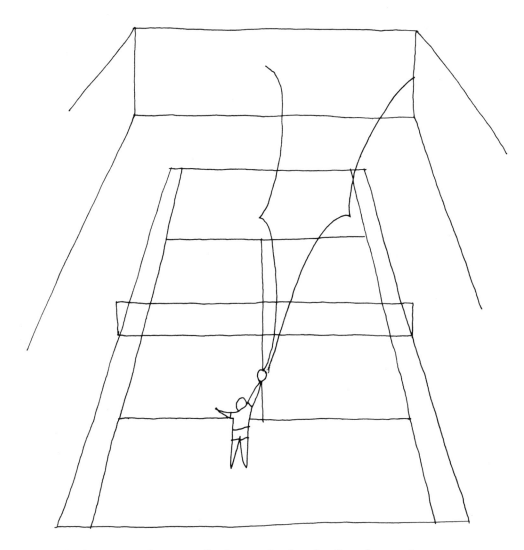

The best targets for most effective overhead and volley placements are the opponents' deep corners or down the middle of the court slightly to the left of center.

deuce court player. Hit the ball hard enough to prevent an attacking shot and with enough pace to get the ball to the back screen. At the same time, hit the ball softly so it does not "set up" off the wires and provide your opponent with the opportunity to make an offensive return. Force the opposition to make a safe return, probably in the form of a backhand lob off the wires. The safe shot can be pulled from your bag of overheads whenever you are in the least bit of trouble, off balance, or somewhat out of position and deep in your own court. This shot will rarely win a point for you (unless the opponent errs), but it will keep you in the point until you get a better chance to make a winner.

So much for playing safe. Granted, it is not much fun, but it is often necessary — even in top-level tournament competition. Assume now your opponent has hit a short lob and you have an opportunity to do something more interesting with the ball. What are your options?

First, before you do anything, talk with your partner to be sure who is going to hit the shot. There is nothing like a "Yours!" or "Mine!" or a "Hit!" or "Out!" to turn a couple of good paddle players into a really effective team. Frequent and loud comunications between teammates can prevent lobs from dropping untouched by either partner — there is nothing worse, more damaging, or humiliating. So, again, first talk or, better yet, *yell* as the ball approaches. Once you know a lob is yours, here are some forcing or winning shots to try:

The High Bounce or Smother Overhead — Hit *down* abruptly on the ball so that it first lands short of the service line, then bounces over

An ideal overhead. The ball should be descending as it goes into the back screen.

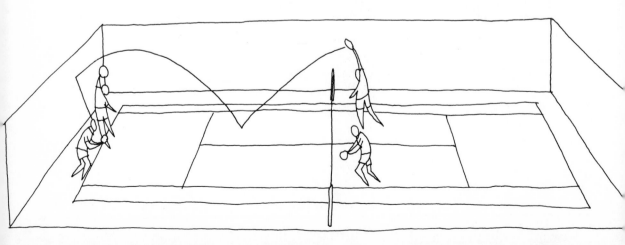

your opponent's head into the corner and dies before hitting the back screen. A winner! But also a difficult shot and a slight gamble since you can misjudge, hit too short, and allow your opponent to return with an offensive overhead of his own from the corner.

The Corner Angle Overhead — Hit down on this shot also but with more angle into the side wire and before your opponent can get to it. The ball then continues off the side wire, upward, out of reach of your opponent's threatening overhead, to its maximum height between the side and back wires. The ball then begins to descend, hitting the back screen ever so gently on the way down, thus making a very difficult shot to return. This is a near winner but is not without its own perils. You can hit the shot too wide in your desire to reach the side wire and make a simple, terrible error as the ball lands beyond the "out" alley line. Or, the ball can "hang" before it gets to the first wire, allowing your opponent to hit an aggressive shot.

The Sweet Spot Overhead — On this shot you actually aim right at the corner —the intersection point between the side and back screens. When you successfully hit this magical spot (the screen's "Sweet Spot"), the ball takes a crazy, unpredictable bounce and you usually have a very satisfying winner. Even when you miss but come close, you are likely to get an unanticipated quick bounce from the corner and you force an error or an even weaker lob from your opponent. This overhead should be hit deeper than the previous two — bouncing on or beyond the service line. It should also be hit with somewhat more pace than most overheads to get more "action" out of the corner if you are fortunate enough to hit that magical spot.

The Overhead Belt or Smash — Here is the one exception to the platform tennis "Don't-Hit-Hard" rule, because your objective is to belt the blazes out of the ball. Your goal is to hit your opponent either directly or as the ball rebounds off the deck — thus winning you the point. The other purpose for applying power to this particular overhead is to attain such a strong bounce off the back wires that your opponent cannot react fast enough to catch up to the ball before it bounds a second time on the playing surface. This shot is hit as deep in the court as possible, and with all the power you can manage. It is a fun shot and a pleasant (and effective) change of pace. Some (more caddish) men have been known to use it very effectively in championship caliber mixed doubles — aiming it, of course, toward the woman's side of the court.

The shot is, however, fraught with much danger. In your exuberance, you can mis-hit, or hit short and into the net, or hit long and over the base line. Also, after caroming off the back screen, the ball can hang in a very precarious position somewhere over the service line, allowing your opponent to return the shot with an overhead at near point blank range. This shot is not recommended for frequent use but when employed serves the purpose of keeping your opponents guessing and a little off balance.

Those are some of the basic shots off the overhead. There are undoubtedly many more variations, which I urge you to try. I strongly recommend that you experiment with different shots of your own from time to time. Variety is one of the special and appealing features of platform tennis. There are as many shots as there are people to dream them up.

4. *Patience* — The overhead is one of the easiest shots in the game, yet it is missed almost as frequently as any other shot. The reason may well be a matter of patience — or the *lack* of it! Somehow, it is very easy to get excited during long points when the ball is "sitting up" and just waiting to be put away. The shot looks so easy and there is so much you can do with it that frequently you forget to be *patient* — to *relax* and to *think*.

Be patient. Wait for the opening. Don't expect to win a point on every shot. Remember, the court is relatively small and the opposition can cover its half quite easily. An outright winner in paddle is a rarity.

Try to relax during those long points. Always be alert for the unexpected, but once that lob is thrown up and you have talked with your partner about whose ball it is, simmer down and keep your composure. You have all the time in the world, and the pressure is really on your opponents. They are at the base line defending. You and your partner have the advantageous net position.

Finally, *think!* This advice applies to *all* aspects of the game. On the overhead, however, you have so many options and so much time that you think more than on other platform tennis shots in which your reflexes and instincts can take over and assist. Conjure up the shot that has the best chance of success, think positive thoughts about how you are going to hit it, then relax and hit it!

If you follow all these tips, practice hard and often, concentrate, and think all the time, you will *still* "blow" an occasional overhead. I sure do. Even my perfect partner John Mangan does. Let's face it, you cannot totally eliminate errors, but by following these precepts, you certainly can minimize them. And that's the "name of the game" — especially in paddle.

In closing, I would like to toast all paddlers, past, present, and future. "May the *last point* always be yours!"

Jesse F. Sammis III, an all-around, versatile athlete, literally dominated
the world of paddle with his partner Gordon Gray between 1966 and
1972. The Greenwich, Connecticut, pair took the National Men's
Doubles title between 1969 and 1971 and were finalists in 1966, 1968,
and 1972. During these years they also won the New Canaan, Rye,
and Greenwich major invitational tournaments. No wonder there was
talk that the "dynasty" should be broken up! "Sam" is also an excellent
court tennis, squash racquets, and tennis competitor. He was an
outstanding performer on the U.S. Olympic Fronton team that competed
in 1968 at Mexico City. His wife Jinny is a fine paddle player, and
they have frequently played together in the National Mixed Doubles
with a good deal of success.

10. | JESSE F. SAMMIS III

Playing the Deuce
or Forehand Court

IF I WERE ASKED to characterize the right-court or deuce-court player's function on a platform tennis court, I would liken it to that of a
guard in basketball. He protects and feeds the big scorer on the team.
The forehand court competitor "sets 'em up for the kill," and most of
the coups de grâce are the responsibility of his partner playing the ad
side of the court. This does *not* mean that the deuce-court player's
only duty is to push the ball back into play. He can still drive forcing
shots, keep the opponents off balance, intimidate his opponent, and
perform all of the functions required to effectively hold up his half of
the court. It's just that the right court does not offer the openings and
angles available to the person in the ad court. Remember, though,
the deuce side is still 50 percent of the court, and, even more than in
tennis, it truly "takes two" to make a winning platform tennis combination.

One of the restricting features for the forehand-court player is the
side screen that frequently impedes him from taking a full, unencum-
bered stroke. A wide-angled cross-court shot, therefore, is practically
impossible to hit. The individual playing the ad court, on the other
hand, has the side screen behind him when executing an offensive forehand. In addition, the right-court player's body is almost always in the
way when he attempts to hit a forehand cross court, whereas the backhand side player's body is rarely an obstruction as he is usually aim-

ing his forehand cross court (to the right) and meeting the ball out front and away from his body.

Off the wires, however, the partner in the deuce court might have a slight advantage when an opportune moment arrives to hit an offensive shot. Usually more pace can be generated off a forehand wire shot than a backhand. When the partner in the ad court is forced to return a screen shot off his backhand he invariably hits a lob.

Opponents' shots that come down the middle of the court should, the majority of the time, be returned by the left-court player. The reason is very simple — he will be making a forehand return. The right-court partner can do very little with a backhand that has to be returned from the center of the base line. Then he, too, will probably have to lob. The backhand side player, however, who should have a good, forcing forehand, at least might have the opportunity to make a more offensive return.

Despite these few inhibiting features the forehand player can still contribute a great deal toward creating a "not-to-be-denied" platform tennis team. After all, he has to hit at least as many service returns, overheads, lobs, serves, volleys, wire shots, etc., as his partner. If he can help win that *first* point of every game when he and his partner are receiving, he can be a tremendous "lift" to his teammate. Paddle is a game of momentum and confidence. By winning the first point the team is mathematically 25 percent of the way toward breaking service and its chances of taking the serve are probably 50 percent better.

Basic Strategy and Tactics — My following comments regarding platform tennis strategy are really axiomatic for *either* the forehand or backhand court players. With the few exceptions and points previously mentioned, the forehand court player's basic objectives and tactics are *identical* to those of his partner in the left court.

1. Concentrate on hitting error-provoking shots that either win the point immediately or produce a setup for you or your ad-court partner to hit a putaway on the next shot.

2. As you are playing you should try to build up confidence in every aspect of your game. This means gaining confidence by hitting every imaginable stroke boldly and aggressively. Mental assurance breeds good shots. Neither a negative attitude nor a fear of trying certain shots will produce a winner.

3. Play all your shots with a purpose behind them. Try to set up shots for your partner's strengths. Make a habit of thinking *two* shots ahead. In other words, don't always go for the outright, one-stroke winner. First you have to "set 'em up" and then make the kill.

4. Imagine two salt shakers positioned diametrically across from each other on a lazy Susan. As the lazy Susan moves the shakers obviously rotate their positions. You and your partner should circulate and cover for each other in much the same manner — thus protecting all parts of the court. For example, if your partner playing the backhand side moves up toward the net and over somewhat into your forehand side of the court, you should move back and over somewhat toward the center to help cover his side if necessary.

5. When ahead, stay with your winning style. When losing, do anything to change the tempo and trend of the match. If you have been continually thwarted in your attempts to take the offensive, play defensively in order to provoke errors and get your rhythm and confidence back. Gordon Gray, my long-time partner, and I advocate even changing court sides when things aren't going our way.

6. Keep constant chatter going between you and your teammate. This lets him know where you are on the court and also keeps the line of communications open so there is little or no hesitation as to who will take the next shot. Always encourage your partner — especially when he is off his game.

7. Always be on the lookout for weaknesses in your opponents and, once discovered, exploit them mercilessly. One player may be volleying well but experiencing difficulties with his overheads. The obvious tactic is to "lob that person to death!" If you feel one of the opponents is getting tired, tell your partner and the two of you should keep playing your shots at the weary one. If the opponents have started bickering, keep the pressure on the player making the most errors, and this will drive them further apart.

Playing the Wires — Learning to play the wires properly is an essential part of the game for two reasons. First, from a defensive standpoint, the wires provide the player with that second chance to return the ball. Specifically, if your opponent hits a good shot that you decide not to take before it bounds into the screening, you have the opportunity and the time to regroup, scamper back, and return the ball without losing the point. Second, the wires can be used to take the offensive. For example, if your opponent hits a shot that comes off the wires above net level, you have an opportunity to "pick a spot" and execute an offensive shot with a putaway or error-provoking stroke.

As a general rule, it is extremely difficult to make a truly offensive shot with a ball that comes off the wires below net level. The reason is that due to the height of the net in relation to the short distance between the net and base line, the ball if hit with pace will invariably sail out beyond the base line. An effective shot to be considered, however, when the ball is below net level and your opponents are standing back from the net (thus precluding the possibility of their hitting a drop volley), is to fake a hard, straight drive and hit a soft "floater." If this shot is properly disguised and executed your opponents, anticipating a lob, will have backed up and therefore will have to hit your ball with their body weight falling away from the ball. Frequently they will pop it out or weakly hit it up in the air for you to pounce on.

When playing the wires, you should always have your paddle back, cocked, and ready to hit the ball. With the paddle back you will find you have more time. You will then play the wires with a fluid, graceful stroke. You should not run to the ball and at the last second take a hurried, jerky swing. There is a beautiful rhythm to screen play! Another important point to help you play the wires effortlessly is to leave plenty of room between the screening and your body. This distance is a question of judgment and experience gained from practice. Stay far enough away from the screens so that your swing is not cramped. When you make contact with the rebounding ball your body should be positioned behind it and you should be able to take a full, uninhibited stroke. It is difficult to return a ball when you find yourself too close to the wires and the ball is coming in toward your body. Also, by keeping a judicious distance from the wires you give yourself a better chance to adjust to the ball that unexpectedly jumps out toward you at the last second.

When it appears possible that a ball will hit dead center in the back corner, the forehand player's responsibility is to cover the side wire and leave the back wire coverage to his backhand partner. This situation does not occur often — and only in top-caliber play — usually only when the opponent has hit a hard overhead at the corner, which does not leave you the time to cover both wires. Your partner should be "playing" every shot with you that goes into your corner in order to protect against the sudden, unpredictable rebound and a possible winner. It can be very upsetting for your opponents to hit the corner for an apparent winner only to have you or your partner return the ball as though it were a routine retrieval.

Playing the wires correctly can keep you in a point or set up a winner. Most of your returns (probably as high as 80 to 90 percent) off the screens should and will be lobs, but the occasion will arise when a ball rebounds high and far enough out into the court to enable you to hit an offensive return. The wires should not be viewed as a last resort. They represent both a second opportunity in defensive play as well as a chance to hit effective, offensive shots.

Return of Service — The return of service is one of the truly golden opportunities in the entire game for the deuce-court player to go for an outright winner, an error-provoking shot, or a return that sets up a winner on the next shot. The key points to remember when returning the serve from the deuce court are

1. Stay low! You should bend your knees and be ready to attack a serve — especially the serve that continually lands short in your service box.

2. Minimize your backswing! On the return of service when you do not have a great deal of time to size up where the ball will bounce, you should cock your arm quickly and minimize the backswing. By abbreviating your stroke you will be able to pounce on the serve with a minimum amount of effort and motion.

3. Hit the ball on the rise! If possible, you should make contact with the ball almost immediately after it bounds off the deck and hit down on it for as low a return as possible. This is an attacking shot and can either be hit cross court, down the middle, or occasionally at the opposing net man (to keep him honest). Mix up your returns to keep the opposition off balance and guessing.

5. Other types of returns. A service return that is great fun to hit and gives tremendous, personal satisfaction when accomplished successfully is the blitz. That is, returning the ball low, following in

behind it, and stroking your opponent's weak return for an outright winner. Blitzing is employed more and more today as players improve their skills and the game becomes more aggressive. The lob return of serve is an excellent and safe shot.

Return of Opponent's Drop Shot — When the deuce-court player prepares to return a well-hit drop shot, he should approach the ball with the paddle ready, in front of his body and in a position to "wrist" or "flick" the ball back. Typically, the opponents will be on top of the net anxiously awaiting the attempt to return their drop shot. His best shot, therefore, is to hit the ball high and retreat immediately to his corner. If he has had to go in so far that there is no time to scamper back, then he should crouch down close to the net and do everything possible not to be hit by his opponents' ball. He should let his partner cover for him until it is safe to return to the base line.

Covering For Your Partner — You should literally "play" every ball hit to your partner as though he was going to miss it and you would have to make the return. This does not mean, however, that you should encroach on his portion of the court. You should be thinking of covering for him for several reasons:

1. When opponents are "working over" your partner, you will stay in the game and not become stagnant or flatfooted. This practice will also hold and increase your concentration.

2. On balls hit toward your partner's corner, his responsibility is to cover the ball bounding out and down the side wire. As mentioned previously, your responsibility is to cover the ball coming out suddenly along the back screen. When you see that your partner is going to cover the side wire, you should move over toward his corner and be ready to cover that back screen for him just in case he gets the "screwy" rebound.

3. On points when your partner decides to blitz, you should anticipate the opponents picking off his drive and trying to hit the ball past him. If your partner is sure you are covering the court behind him, it will enable him to let the ball go so you can put it back in play. It will also provide him with time to return to his base line position without having to make an especially difficult and undesirable shot that could result in a needless error.

Physical Conditioning — Because I am constantly being accused of being such a "nut" on the subject, I can't help concluding my chapter on something I feel very strongly about, namely, physical fitness. One of the most important pluses for a winning team is physical conditioning. Being in excellent shape has frequently been the "scale tipper" when opposing teams are otherwise evenly matched in all other departments.

There are six exercises I try to do every day of my life. To what degree you wish to pursue them depends on how serious you want to play paddle. If you are highly competitive and wish to play serious platform tennis, doing these daily exercises will pay high dividends. If, on the other hand, you just play once or twice a week "for fun" and socially, then the exercise attained from merely playing is probably adequate.

1. Running — Two to three miles per week is great for the legs and lungs. For a month immediately preceding the Nationals I jog as much as three miles a day.
2. Jumping Jacks — These are essentially deep knee bends and leaping straight up from a semisitting position to a standing one. You are getting in good condition if you can do fifty of these each day.
3. Hand Gripper — Squeeze either a platform tennis ball or a regular hand gripper 100 times.
4. Jumping Rope — A great exercise for improving your wind, strengthening your legs, and sharpening your overall coordination and reflexes. Two to three minutes each day are sufficient.
5. Push-ups — Work toward thirty.
6. Sit-ups — Work toward fifty.

You now know all my "secrets." If you have a definite preference for the forehand or deuce side of the court, play it! Practice often and try to stay with the same partner. Keep yourself in good physical and mental condition. Remember, behind every great doubles player, be he a forehand or backhand side player, there is usually a great doubles *partner!*

Gordon S. Gray, one of the few active players to win the coveted
APTA Honor Award, is one of the all-time great platform tennis
players. Teamed with Ann Symmers from his hometown of Greenwich,
Connecticut, he won the National Mixed Doubles title three years in a
row, 1966–1968. He and his friend Jesse Sammis annexed three
consecutive U.S. Championships in 1969–1971. Sammis and Gray were
virtually unbeatable for six years. Mild-mannered and gentle off the
court, "The Cobra" is the essence of concentration and intense
combativeness in tournament play.

11. | GORDON S. GRAY

Playing the Ad
or Backhand Court

FOR THE RIGHT-HANDED PLAYER in the ad (advantage) court the major opportunity available is the wide-ranging use of an attacking forehand. The style of the game as it's played today is more oriented to the attack than it used to be. While the premium on errorless play will always be important, there is now more emphasis on winning points as opposed to waiting for an opponent's error. Players in the backcourt are constantly seeking ways to draw out the weak return in order to attack it and win the point outright, take the net, or set up the winning shot. The ad-court position gives the person playing that side a large expanse of court open to the forehand drive with the opportunity of scoring or attacking with a follow-up net rush.

I don't want anyone to assume the deuce-court player is not important to the attack. The point is that with two right-handed players the deuce-court player is more restricted by the side wire in his forehand range when both players are in the backcourt. So the ad-court player has far more opportunities to return a wide angle shot off the forehand.

The ability of the ad-court player to range over the space available depends on his ability to anticipate the placement of the opponent's shot. Position yourself close to the alley. If a ball is aimed at your corner you can often cut it off by advancing toward the net and taking it on your forehand. You purposefully leave the middle open and invite the "safe" return. Then, reading your opponent's eyes, position, and paddle movement, move over to the middle and toward the net to attack the "safe placement" and follow your return to the net for the putaway or, at least, to pressure your opponents into the desired error.

A word of caution. These attacking drives and anticipatory attacks can lead you into trouble when the ball does not come where you expected or when it comes too hard, too deep, or too low for you to make your attacking shot with a reasonable margin for error. Don't force the winner — don't attack unless you have the shot you want. If you are attacking down the middle or poaching and the ball isn't where you want it, let it go by and let your partner put up a lob. If you are in your own alley and make a move toward the net and you don't like the ball — stop, turn around, and put up a lob off the wires. If you are caught in too far to go back and hit the ball off the wires, try to get it back into play while recovering. Work for the shot you want and if you don't get it, don't force it, just wait for a better chance. In general, try not to attack a ball below the level of the net. The odds are against you. When you are attacking you want to be able to hit down on the ball.

A word about poaching. If the forehand can reach a shot down the middle he should take it. It doesn't matter on the defensive shots but on the attack the partner with the forehand stroke takes the ball anywhere and any time he has the shot he wants.

In playing the rear corner wires in the ad court, I prefer to back away from the corner and take the ball on my backhand. I find this method less restrictive than positioning myself in the corner and turning with the ball to hit with my forehand. A backhand shot allows me to move my weight forward, brings me closer to the net, and also permits me to see the whole court. But it's a matter of preference. Ted Winpenny almost always turns with the ball and his control is superb. With either method, or in either court, you are primarily going to try to do one of two things: (1) hit a defensive lob to get into position or (2) hit an offensive lob to try to gain the net. With both shots you should know where you are trying to place the ball. Remember that the spot on the court your opponent has to return your lob to will then determine the angle of his return and you should be working for the return you want for a crack at the offensive shot. If you are in trouble in the corner try to lob straight ahead — and vastly reduce your op-

Gordon Gray in one of his most characteristic positions. He has just hit a low, hard forehand from the backhand side of the court and is moving in for what he hopes will be a successful blitz.

ponent's angle back into your corner. By the same token, when your partner lobs straight ahead look for the angle into your corner, and if it's a deep forcing lob be ready to attack the return. If you have a ball you can really lob well and want it to be returned into your corner, lob cross court. If you want to try to get the center shot lob more down the middle.

One more word about taking the ball off the screens. Unless you get a high ball well out from the screen and toward the direction of the net, do not try to drive a winner. The better your opponents the more obvious this word of advice. Too many of us see (or feel) John Mangan winning point after point on this shot and wonder why we don't score as often without realizing that most of us don't have the strength, the overspin, or the control John enjoys. The shot is a good one but not if pressed. Again, wait for the shot you want before you hit an attacking drive. Try faking the drive and hit the forcing lob to set up a better opportunity. Platform tennis is a game of patience!

Volleys and overheads are pretty much the same for either side of the court but the return of serve gives the ad-court player the same advantage on his forehand as the drive. Position yourself close to the side screen and be ready to charge the serve anticipating the server's placement. Give the server the middle of the court but be ready to swoop over. If the serve beats you down the middle let it go by and take it off the wire. If the serve doesn't give you the opportunity you really like — too deep, too far toward the backhand corner — don't force the attack, play it safe and try to set up something for the next shot.

The backhand — I can't think of any right-handed ad-court player who scores consistently with backhand drives. The message is clear — lob the ball off your backhand and try to set up your forehand. There are the obvious exceptions for set-ups, but in general it's a good rule to follow.

Never having been left-handed I can't write about how it feels to play that way, but I can make observations about playing against the lefty in the ad court. You have to be especially careful of the corner wire shot. Feeding a lefty in the corner invites him to move in and crack the ball or take it off two wires and crack it with his forehand. Usually the lefty in the ad court will have a right-handed partner and that makes the middle safe (they will both be hitting backhands) so use it. But when that big forehand does come booming, the man directly in front of him at net takes prime responsibility for his alley and leaves the middle to his partner. Those lefties love to come zinging straight ahead out of their corner. Cut off and protect the alley, let your partner cover the middle, and leave him the far alley for an occasional great shot.

A word about tactics. You are trying to take the flow of the game away from your opponents. You pound away at their weaknesses. You are constantly trying to move them back from the net, trying to force them to hit a ball you can attack but not giving them any errors in the process. If they feel the pressure they will make more errors than usual. But what do you do when this strategy does not work? In the excitement of the game, particularly under tournament pressure, this is a tough problem. The tendency is just to try harder, hit the ball harder, run faster, etc. If you are still getting clobbered you better change tactics fast or the match is over. I'm a poor example, for when Sam Sammis and I are beaten we are usually wiped off the court in straight sets — still trying to get the original game plan going. Somehow, before you find yourself shaking hands with the winners you have to change your tactics. Forget the offense for a while — lob, try to get your timing back — lob, look more closely at the ball — lob, don't let yourself get discouraged and give up — lob again, and by all means talk to your partner. If you really want to try a shakeup, change court sides with your partner for a set. Do anything that changes the game plan. Try to buy time to get your game on the right track. Then go back to the offense.

A word about playing conditions. The hotter the weather or the more slippery the court the more difficult it is to drive the ball hard and the "safer" you have to play. Adjust your game to the conditions — they won't adjust to you.

Finally, the backhand court side is, in my judgment, the *opportunity* side. For the reasons previously stated, the backhand- or ad-court player has more opportunities to do something with the ball. He (or she) has more (and wider) angles to shoot for. In addition, it seems that more pivotal or crucial points (ad in or ad out) occur on this side of the paddle court. If you are comfortable playing the ad court, make certain to take *advantage* of your openings and opportunities!

Editor's Note: Because the right-hander playing the ad court does have many opportunities to "crack" the low, hard cross-court forehands at the server coming up to the net, several teams have recently adopted a defense that seems to make sense and often works. It is commonly known in tennis as "The Australian Shift," but Doug Russell and I were the first to employ it on a paddle court.

When serving to the opponent in the ad court the net man assumes the "ready" position just to the *left* of the center line — the normal distance from the net — with his body turned slightly sideways so that his left shoulder is facing the receiver. His paddle should be up and somewhat to the forehand side. In effect he has firmly planted himself to cut off the opposing ad-court player's big weapons — the forehand down the middle or the wide-angled, hard cross-court return. He is set, ready for it, and can usually volley the ball quite effortlessly off his forehand. When employing the normal formation the server has to handle this difficult return, frequently while still moving in toward the net and off a backhand volley.

The server makes his delivery from a position closer to the center of the court rather than way over to the left. His responsibility when moving in to join his partner is to cover the down-the-alley return, which he is able to do with a forehand volley.

This "Squires' Shift" in platform tennis has worked quite well for Doug and myself and the theory is certainly sound. It does take practice, however, and prearranged, behind-the-back signals allow the net man to poach occasionally. This can be a very disconcerting tactic to the opposition. You get them concentrating on trying to outguess you, or worrying about the possibility of an upcoming "switch," instead of just returning the ball to a particular spot.

This formation actually is inviting the opposing ad-court player to hit down the line, a shot that is nowhere nearly as effective as the wide cross court.

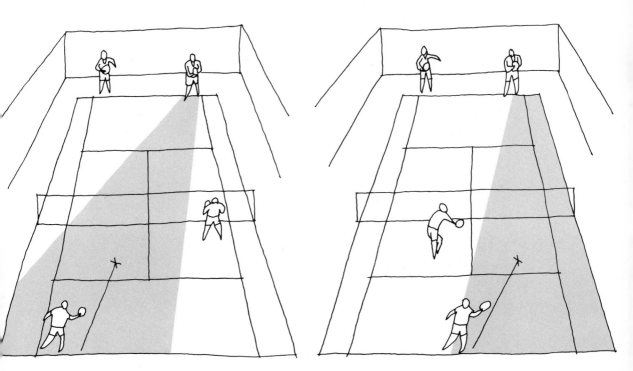

The normal line-up of the serving team when serving to the opponents'
ad court (1.) versus the Squires' Shift (r.). In the Squires' Shift, the
net man is slightly turned sideways, his left shoulder toward the backhand
court opponent. The area open to the opposing ad-court player is
greatly reduced.

Charles F. Baird and his usual partner, Roger Lankenau, have been formidable adversaries against all the high-ranking (and usually younger!) teams. A senior vice president of International Nickel Company of Canada, Ltd., and former under secretary of the navy, Chuck — when teamed with Roger — has been ranked in the Top Ten since 1962. In 1970 he and Dwight Lowell won the New Jersey State Men's Doubles, and in 1971 and 1972 he and his young son "Chip" teamed up to take the State Men's title. In 1972, 1973, and 1974 he and Ned Swanberg won the National Seniors' title. In 1974 he and Roger won the National 45-year-olds' crown — when Chuck was seven years over the limit! It appears that "Papa" Baird and his attractive wife of twenty-seven years Norma have reared a paddle dynasty. Their two sons, Chip and Steve, both former National Boys' champions and in their early twenties, are currently ranked among the top four teams in the nation. Their daughter Nancy (seventeen) was runner-up in the 1973 National Girls' Doubles. Chuck claims he still holds the record for the "longest distance traveled to the Nationals." In 1963, he flew from Paris to Fox Meadow to compete.

12. | CHARLES F. BAIRD

Screen Play

THE SCREENS are what give the great game of platform tennis its unique quality and, at the same time, its most intriguing challenge. In paddle the rear and side screens are one-inch hexagonal galvanized wire that is uniformly tensioned for true rebounding characteristics.

How to play the screens or wires represents the greatest problem to the new platform tennis player. The seasoned tournament player, conversely, is more concerned about his forehand return of service, his serve, or his volleying. For the most part he has become comfortable "playing the wires." Yet, many matches are won or lost by the quality of the defensive and offensive wire play. Offensive play off the screening is for the more expert competitor. The beginner should concern himself with simply (actually not so simply!) getting the ball back across the net — probably by lobbing.

The cardinal principle for the novice to keep in mind is that the wires are his protector and his "best friend." They nullify the power shots of the better players and enable a player to prolong rallies and even to win points from a defensive position if his opponent errs. This concept, strangely enough, often is more easily understood and grasped by the inexperienced racquet player than the good tennis player. The latter has the instinctive feeling that a ball hit through or by him is automatically a point lost. He is likely to stab desperately at the opponent's smash as it goes by, often spoiling his or his partner's chance to play the ball off the wires with little or no effort.

Mig Simpson gracefully retrieves the ball off the wires.

The three most frequent wire shots are: (1) those directly off the back wire, (2) those that strike first on the back wire and bounce into the side wire, and (3) those that hit the side wire first and then bounce off the back wire. There are two other screen shots with which you will have to cope, but not as frequently: (1) those that rebound directly parallel to, and slide along, the side wire and die and those that hit directly in either back corner or "crack" and bounce out crazily.

It is very important to keep in mind that the beginner has far more time than he might think when retrieving balls off the wires. In a word, "Wait!" There really is time to spare on most balls hit with reasonable pace. Learn how to position yourself. Avoid the ball coming right at you and move into position for an uncramped, smooth stroke on your return. Set your feet so that you are stroking from a solid foundation.

Watch your opponent's stance and stroke carefully to anticipate where, and how hard, he will be hitting his shot. Most players at the backcourt stand just inches behind the base line and, depending on the speed of the opponent's shot and tautness of the wires, move toward or away from the wires to make the return.

Let's initially discuss the basic shot to the *back wire*. Here all my comments are concerned only with *defensive* returns. Assume you are playing the left or backhand side of the court and are returning a ball with your forehand that is rebounding off the back screen and down the middle. Turn sideways to the ball as it goes past you and, with a stiff wrist, swing up and out toward the net as you make contact with the ball. Try to hit the ball at a comfortable height — somewhere between the knees and waist and, when possible, slightly out in front of you — as you normally try to do on all regular ground strokes. Don't rush. Move and stroke with a relaxed motion. There is a beautiful rhythm to screen play that once acquired is easily retained.

On the *back-to-side-wire* ball on the left side of the court, avoid letting it touch you as it goes past, then move quickly to the side wire and wait for the ball to rebound — with your paddle back. Don't rush your shot or scrape at the ball as it hits high on the screening. As the ball comes off the wires allow it to drop to the preferred height or even below knee level before you attempt your return, which will often be a lob.

Better players will often hit their overheads so the balls will bounce high on the *side wire* and spin *into the back wire*. These are probably the most difficult screen shots for the beginner, who has to make a choice. One style is to follow the ball around, facing first the side wire, then the back. From the left side of the court the player is then in a position to hit a forehand return. John Mangan and many other better players prefer this approach. It permits them to decide at the last moment whether to lob or hit an offensive forehand shot should the ball come out far enough. Gordon Gray, on the other hand, seems to be just as effective backing up and returning practically all side/back wire shots off his backhand. Virtually all right-court players back away from the ball as it comes off the two wires and return off their

A.   B.

A. A player moves paddle up and back as he goes into screening to retrieve the ball, which has already gone past him.

B. His body is positioned sideways to net as he concentrates on the ball and moves paddle down and low.

C.   D.   E.

C. The player keeps the paddle face open to hit a lob. His body weight
is beginning to move forward.

D. When possible, contact between paddle and ball is made in front of the
body. The player must bend his knees in order to meet the low, dying
ball.

E. The player's followthrough is full and high to give both height and
depth to the lob.

forehands. This method allows the player to always be aware of his opponents' positions. In either case, it is important when hitting the side/back wire return never to make contact with the ball when your back is to the net. You will never be able to hit an effective offensive shot from such an awkward position. Whether you back up or turn with the ball is entirely up to you. Either method is correct and both have certain advantages as well as disadvantages. Whichever you can do more easily and effectively is the proper one for you.

On the balls that slide along the side wire and die, the best approach is to try to "scrape" or "wipe" the ball off the wire with a fairly loose wrist. In other words, run the edge of your paddle along the screen — don't try to "pick" the ball off.

When the ball hits the corner where back and side screens intersect, *both* you and your partner must be alert and prepared to play the ball, as it may rebound out toward the middle or toward your teammate's side of the court. Tournament players retrieve a high percentage of these balls that rebound unpredictably.

Really and truly the only way to learn to play the wires effectively and gracefully is to practice. To learn the angles, how varying speeds affect angles, to understand the deception employed by different opponents, to learn proper court positioning, to learn when to hit an offensive shot and, above all, to employ patience can only be accomplished by practice and experience. Try to practice against better players. Practice with your partner (who will, in turn, be practicing his overheads). It's worth it, as a good screen player can make any opponent work hard to win points and, in so doing, can also win many himself!

The following are generalities that apply to all screen players. About 90 percent of screen shots should be *lobs*. The offensive 10 percent should be executed only when the percentage of success is high. Again, don't rush your shots. The longer you lob, the more the opponents have to work hitting overheads and moving back and then in toward the net after every overhead. This action tires them and ultimately creates openings. Wait until you have driven them back with a particularly deep lob and when their return is either short in your court or else very hard off the screen, then you can hit an offensive, forcing shot and go into the net. Hit your forcing shot with precision, power, and topspin to draw a weak return. Occasionally the more expert player will get a chance to hit a "screen overhead" off the right side wire. It's a devastating shot that rakes the opponents' court and rattles their composure, but the ball must be hanging high and be out far enough from the back screen to provide such a "juicy" setup.

Body position is the most important factor on all wire shots. An adroit screen player will really hustle to get into a position that leaves him the greatest number of options. Good body position allows a variety of shots and thus a good deal of deception. Only the beginner or the tired player will find himself hitting a screen shot too close to his body, or taking last-second flicks at the ball, or making relatively simple returns appear to be very difficult.

One final word. While the purpose of this chapter has been to describe the basic principles of screen play and *using* the wires, many of the better tournament players, whenever possible and when they are comfortable doing so, will "cut off" shots *before* the balls go into the screening. A ball that is slowing up and dying or one that just might be going directly toward that back corner for a possible winner, should be blocked off and returned before bounding into the screening. For example, occasionally you will have the opportunity to hit an overhead from the backcourt. Unless you are certain of your overhead, resist the temptation. The chance may occur, however, because your opponent, in attempting to obtain a high bounce over your head and into your back corner, doesn't get the ball high enough. With such a weak overhead, or a "tired," mushy ball, your opponent has hit a shot that sits up at just about service height. Bang it! Go for your winner. Don't let it pass by you and into the screen.

Again, it is a question of judgment gained personally through experience and practice. If you are relaxed and feel comfortable in hitting regular ground strokes from deep in your court, then do it! After all, you are giving your opponents less time than they have when they force you to hit a great many wire shots. On the other hand, you also have less time on your returns when you don't employ the wires. Remember, the screens are there and they are an integral and distinctive part of the game. Use them! Next to your partner, they are your greatest ally and asset on the court.

Dwight E. Lowell II, at thirty-two one of the outstanding left-handers in the game today, with Bradley Drowne was part of the third nationally ranked team in 1971 and 1972. During these two years, he and Brad won the New Jersey State, Buffalo, Rye, and Cleveland Invitationals, and twice they were semifinalists in the National Men's. Dwight has a strong forehand return of service and a fine backhand volley. Only after a good deal of experimentation has he finally decided that a left-handed paddler should definitely play the deuce side of the court. He was a member of the U.S. Fronton Team that competed in the World's Championship at San Sebastian, Spain, in 1970.

13. | DWIGHT E. LOWELL II

Advantages and Disadvantages
for the Left-Handed Player

AMONG THE TOP TEN nationally ranked teams of the 1972 season, five consisted of left-handed players teamed with right-handers. On four of the teams the lefty played the left or ad court.

The growing exposure and popularity of platform tennis has, over the past several years, attracted many younger players, in addition to a large number of very fine tennis and squash players. Although consistency of play is undoubtedly still the determining factor in paddle, power, quickness, and aggressive play are beginning to dominate the game. As a result, left-handers are starting to consider switching to the deuce side of the court. Until now, lefties almost automatically chose or were assigned to the ad court because of their seemingly more natural ease in handling screen play, as they play the wire shots off the forehand.

Let's weigh the pros and cons of the left-handed paddler playing the ad and deuce courts and assume in both cases his partner is right-handed. The most obvious difference and advantage of the lefty being in the ad court is that both partners are hitting forehands off the corner wires. Therefore, the great advantage of a lefty in the ad court is that both teammates are in the enviable position of being able to hit more offensive shots from the corners. Right-handers playing the ad court are usually forced to retrieve a barrage of wire shots with their back-

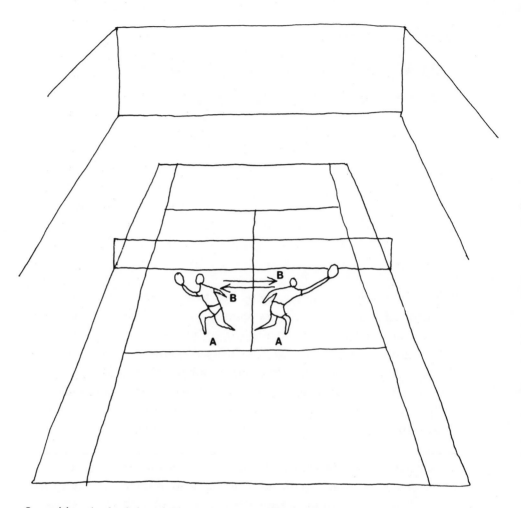

In position A, the lefty/righty team has backhands down the middle of
the court, which is awkward and undesirable. After switching to
position B, both players can return volleys and overheads down the
center with their forehands.

hands. Unlike tennis, the backhand in paddle is almost always a defensive shot designed merely to keep the ball in play or, at best, to force the opposition out of position with a deep lob.

However, the lefty's strength in the ad court introduces a potential weakness to his team — the middle of the court. When the opposing team is serving and thereby gaining the advantage of the net, most of the time their obvious strategy is to volley and return overheads to the middle of the backcourt. The lefty and his partner are, therefore, compelled to hit only backhands. This is one reason why the automatic placement of the southpaw in the ad court has recently been questioned. Teams are weighing the trade-off between having two players who can both hit offensive wire shots from the corners and teammates who have to hit backhands whenever the ball lands in the center portion of the court — including the shots retrieved off the back screen.

Lefty-righty combinations invariably have longer matches because of the rallies that develop as the opposing team continually hits the ball down the middle, a "safe" but prolonging style of play.

The lefty's primary responsibility when playing the ad court is to position himself so that he forces his opponents into hitting either an overhead or volley to his or his teammate's forehand. He must exploit offensive opportunities whenever possible, which means hitting aggressive shots when either his or his partner's lobs result in the opponents' returning a weak overhead to his forehand.

A left-hander has a natural disadvantage when returning serves from the ad court. It is difficult for him to "hide" his backhand and, as a result, he is frequently off balance or hitting from a cramped position. In addition, the lack of a wide angle makes the usually effective cross-court return of serve more difficult to hit. A right-hander returning serves from the ad court cannot only protect his backhand but can easily hit cross court over the net at its lowest height.

In my opinion, a lefty's most effective service return from the ad court is one that is hit hard and directly at the opposing net man or one that is hit down the middle. These two spots provide the best angle and an element of surprise. By concentrating on these areas, the lefty can keep the net man honest and prevent him from cutting off an occasional cross-court service return. In essence, the lefty has the same rather limited choice of shots when returning serve from the ad court that the right-hander has when playing the deuce side. A good rule of thumb for a lefty returning serve from the ad court is to hit at the net man when the serve lands wide to the forehand and to hit down the middle when the serve crowds him toward the center.

When a lefty/righty team is serving and thus gaining the net immediately on nearly all points, the style and strategy of their play, with one exception, is really quite orthodox. The one move a lefty must make when playing the net is to position himself as quickly as possible to the *right* side of his partner. The importance of this court positioning becomes readily apparent the first time the opponents hit a deep lob down the middle, and if the lefty is not on the deuce side of the court both teammates can only return lobs by hitting *backhand* overheads. This is a very difficult and normally weak shot, which the opponents will undoubtedly exploit time and again — if given the chance. Very few players possess the strength or accuracy to hit an effective backhand overhead. The lefty is at net on the left or "wrong" side of the court whenever his partner is serving to the deuce opponent, or when he himself comes to net following his serve to the opponents' ad court.

The left-hander can correct the positioning problem when he finds himself to the left of his partner at net by switching court sides early in the playing of a point. This can easily be accomplished by either partner yelling "Switch!" before or after he has hit a ball that will require a little time for the opponents to reach and return. A good rule of thumb is to switch on the first easy overhead. The overhead should, however, be hit deep to the middle wire or deep and with a good deal of angle to the opponents' wire. Such shots provide both teammates with enough time to switch court sides and be properly positioned to continue playing without being caught off balance by an alert opponent who is aware of the upcoming switch and will try to take advantage of it. By being on the right side of the court as often as possible, the center of the lefty/righty's court is then covered by both partner's forehands.

After several years of experimenting with different partners and playing both sides of the court, I have personally come to the conclusion that the advantages of the left-hander playing the *deuce* side exceed the disadvantages. With platform tennis becoming more and

Al Collins (l.), a southpaw, and Bob Kingsbury are properly positioned
to cover the middle with their forehands.

more an aggressive game, the lefty has more opportunities to be offensive from the right-court side.

On the return of serve, which is one of the few shots that offers the hitter a chance to go for an outright winner, or a forcing shot that often provokes an error from the opponents, the southpaw in the deuce court has the same wider angles and openings that the righty has in the ad court.

In the deuce court the lefty can protect or "hide" his backhand allowing only the very best servers to place the ball in such a way as to make him return with a backhand from an off-balance position. To me, this is the real strength of a lefty/righty team. *Both* teammates are in a position to exert tremendous pressure on their opponents' serves.

A lefty (playing the deuce court) teamed with a righty provides the best possible combination for returning serves effectively and for attacking their opponents' volleys. Again, because this formation has two forehands down the middle, the opposition is faced with the difficulty of trying to volley to backhands that are almost nonexistent. The natural position for the lefty is to crowd his side wire with his back and "hide" his backhand. The lefty will quickly learn where he should best position himself to be able to cut off as many returns as possible before the balls bound into the side wire, forcing him to back up and return screen shots defensively off his backhand.

There's another reason why I feel it is better strategy for a left-hander to play the forehand side of the court. In the deuce court perhaps only as little as 20 percent of the court area is open for the opponents to hit a "safe" or effective placement, that is, one that has to be returned with a backhand. The opponents only have two small areas to aim for from which an offensive shot can only occasionally be made. This restriction on a team's ability to "play" a larger area of the court places a great deal of pressure on an opposing team — both psychologically as well as in actual performance. Such a limited target often causes errors. The team playing against the lefty/righty duo will frequently hit wide and out when attempting to crowd or hit for the opponents' backhands.

In addition, by playing the deuce court the lefty is bound to get more opportunities for both him and his partner to hit high-percentage offensive forehand drives. Since balls landing in 80 percent of the court area will be to his or his partner's forehands, he can afford to be more patient and wait for just the right shot he or his partner feel most confident hitting. On the other hand, when playing the ad court, where most balls are aimed down the "fat" (center) part and must be returned off the backhands, the team must take more chances when the rare forehand opportunity is presented.

Paddle is, after all, mostly a game of percentages, and the team that usually wins is the team that plays consistently, forces errors, and takes chances only when it is hitting its best shots. With two forehands in the middle of the court, the lefty/righty team can certainly be more consistent, force more errors, and still obtain more opportunities to execute its best shots — all because its forehands are covering a majority of the court area.

C. Michael O'Hearn, Jr., is an insurance broker, father of four children, and a Yale graduate. Mike's greatest platform tennis accomplishment occurred in 1965 when he and Tom Holmes upset Ted Winpenny and Dick Squires in the finals to win the National Men's Doubles. Despite major back surgery, he is still a fine player. In February 1974 he and Willard Heminway beat Jesse Sammis and Gordon Gray in the New Canaan Invitational — a feat he had not been able to achieve when he was at the peak of his form. He states he is one of the highest handicapped paddler/golfers in the east — third only to John Mangan and Dave Jennings.

14. | C. MICHAEL O'HEARN, JR.

Winning Strategy in Men's Doubles

IT'S BEEN SO LONG since I have won a doubles tournament of any consequence that I am not sure if I have sufficient recall to write meaningfully on the subject. My apologies in advance, therefore, if my elephantine memory squeaks at times.

Before delving into the fundamentals of playing and winning in good men's doubles, I would like to talk a little about a quality that makes the difference between winning and losing a close match, between winning a sixty-four-team draw tournament and losing along the way "to some team you should have beaten." The difference is *attitude*.

How often have you "played over your head"? Made impossible shots? Played virtually errorless paddle? Never let the other team get started? On the other hand, how often have you not been able to really get going? Missed easy shots? Not felt as if you were on top of your game and really in the match? Given two teams of approximate ability, the team with the proper, positive attitude, the confidence, the team with the adrenal glands pumping will invariably win. If both teams are so inspired, there should be some darn good paddle to watch — and you will see "swings," or changes in momentum. One team will be down five games to two and will fight back to tie the score at five-all. Maybe then the other team, having seen a big lead disappear, will mentally "dig in," causing the momentum to change in

Mike O'Hearn (l.) and Oliver Kimberly, both former National titlists, display the poise and concentration needed to win.

its direction. It will take the next two games to close out the set.

A number of factors can cause a change in momentum. It could be a particular point such as a let cord, a double fault, a great (or lucky) shot, a flagrant error, a bad line call, or simply the ability to grab hold mentally when the chips are down and make the shot that wins the all-important point. The great platform tennis players and teams, without exception, have had this *mental control* — the concentration, the drive, the positive attitude to complement their physical execution of shots.

Picking a partner may sound corny, but it is ever so important. During the season you will occasionally see one of the better teams split up for a tournament and play with other players of equal ability.

Invariably when they come up against a *team* (two players who have played a good deal in tournaments together), the two individuals comprising the pickup team will lose. Factors such as not having played together under the pressure of competition, not having the "feel" for each other, and lacking the proper attitude all play an important role and contribute to their downfall.

More often than not a bigger deterrent, however, will be that their individual styles and personalities do not complement each other. The new "team" may have two aggressive or leader-type players, or two back-up men, in which case no one takes the lead. Look at the good teams that have won the Nationals in the past few years, such as John Mangan and Bob Kingsbury. John is the aggressive player, hitting the winning shots, while Bobby seldom errs, keeps the ball in play, retrieves exceptionally well, and sets up John for his big forehand. The team of Jesse Sammis and Gordon Gray is another excellent example. Gordon, again the aggressive partner with a fine forehand, makes the winner or forced error while Jesse supports him beautifully with a steady, get-everything, set-'em-up-style of play. With few exceptions (a notable one is John Beck and Herb FitzGibbon, the 1974 Men's Doubles Champions) there must be one of each type to comprise a great team, and the aggressive player almost always plays the *backhand* court. For a right-handed backhand-court player the forehand is in the middle and he can more easily control and pick the spots from that side.

Most left-handed players play the backhand or ad court. I will not say this is wrong, but I happen to believe it is difficult for a lefty to be aggressive from the backhand court. I think he has a better chance of being a more offensive player from the forehand (deuce) court, where his forehand is in the middle. He therefore gets the same advantages as a right-handed player does in the ad court.

If you were a platform tennis buff in 1965, you may recall that Tommy Holmes and I played Ted Winpenny and Dick Squires in the finals of the Nationals. (Ted and Dick won the following year.) Our best strategy was for me to play the steady role — return serves low — and for Tommy to charge the net and try to put their first volley away, which he did time and time again. Tommy also had the ability to attack an opponent's overhead if the opponent tried to bounce the ball over his head in the corner. He would step in and give them an over-head right back while I stood by and applauded. Tommy attacked and I tried to back him up and support him with steadiness. This strategy worked for us and it will work for you.

I will divert here because this particular match was an excellent example of attitude and a swing of momentum. At the break we were behind two sets to one. Tommy was down in the dumps mentally and looking like he might remain there until he had a short talk with Dick Hebard and Zan Carver, two of the all-time great players, since re-tired. In essence their pep talk told him to attack and to play to win. Tommy came out for the fourth set like an ignited firecracker and we won in five sets.

In a nutshell, analyze your own game and style. What do you do best and naturally? Are you the aggressive-type player who likes to take charge and can make winners, or are you the player who is hap-pier just hanging in there, making few errors, getting balls back, and hitting shots that you hope your opponents will return weakly for your partner to attack? Then look around for someone who is willing to play the opposite role. If you are unable to find a partner who nicely complements your game, at least find one who is *better* than you! This is a game of headwork — not just footwork — and a little preseason headhunting sometimes makes up for midseason miseries.

Now that you are a team, play like one and stay together. Knowing what your partner will do, and when he will do it, takes years of prac-tice, much competitive play, and a good deal of talking back and forth — both during and after points. Generally speaking, you stay together, either both in the backcourt or both at net. Usually each player covers his half of the court, and the forehand (if there is one down the center) hits the returns that land in the middle.

All rules, however, are made to be broken. Sometimes one player will attack from the backcourt — perhaps on a weak serve or a short volley. When he does, his partner should immediately move to the center of the backcourt in an I-formation, just as in football. He should not charge toward the net with his partner, but act as a backup should his partner's foray falter or fail. If the opponents volley your teammate's shot through or past him, you should be in a position to have a chance to reach the ball and throw up a lob in order to give

Doug Russell (l.) and Dick Squires congratulate each other at the end
of a tournament match. Fierce, competitive play is invariably followed
by warm camaraderie and lasting friendships between partners and
opponents alike.

your partner time to retreat. If your partner is successful in driving
the ball through the opposition, then rush up to join him in case one
of the opponents retrieves the ball off the wires.

Another situation in which you should leave your normal position
(playing your half of the court) will occur after your opponents have
hit a very deep lob to your partner. When your partner goes back and
perhaps hits a short overhead, the opposition will probably hit their
next shot at his feet. Anticipate this shot; leave your position at net,
crossing over to your partner's side, and attempt to cut off the return.
At the same time your partner should cross over to the position you
just left. In other words, instances will frequently arise where you and
your partner will have to help each other out.

Just as in tennis, as soon as you step onto the court to rally and
warm up before the match, start sizing up your opponents. Even better, if you know who the opposition will be, watch them play part of
their previous match. Look for their weaknesses and their strengths.
See how they react to certain shots. Ask people who have played

them before what is the best way to beat them. In other words, do a little "homework" by scouting your opponents. If one of them charges the net extremely fast after serving, he should be vulnerable to a lob. The same is true of anyone who stands very close to the net in the volleying position. If one of them is slow getting in on his serve, drop the ball at his feet. If a net man poaches often, keep him honest by hitting some balls down the line a few times. Generally, keep alert, use your head, and mercilessly attempt to exploit the opposition's weaknesses.

I have discussed attitude. Another important ingredient of top-flight platform tennis is *patience*. Most points in paddle are won on *errors* — a much larger percentage than in tennis. An informal survey of several championship matches involving the best players was recently made and the statistics proved that about 85 percent of the points were won on the other team's errors! It makes sense to somehow get the ball over the net and let the other guy make the mistake. 'Don't try to knock the stuffing out of the ball. First, there isn't any stuffing, and, second, you will be a consistent loser.

If, however, you have the opportunity to take the offense, do it! You will never beat the "big boys" by only being patient. If your opponent hits a weak volley, or a short serve, or an overhead that is either too short or so hard that it bounces high and far out from the screen, take advantage of it. Return hard and low down the middle or down the alley. In other words, be patient, but be waiting for the opportunity. It will eventually come, so be sure you take full advantage of it.

In platform tennis, as in life, the players are creatures of habit. Given the same shot, most players will return the ball the same way to the same spot everytime. If a player happens to have the most formidable forehand return in the game, maybe he can get away with hitting it hard every time, but let's face it, you don't and I don't. So mix up your shots. Keep your opponents off balance. Keep them guessing which shot you might hit next. Let's assume you are playing me and can hit my serve pretty well. You are returning it consistently and effectively down the middle and low. Pretty soon I adjust and start coming in faster and crowding over toward the middle. I am adapting myself to your return of service. Suddenly you throw up a lob as I charge the net looking for your usual low drive down the center.

If it is a very deep lob, I might not be able to stop in time to hit an overhead. I therefore have to go back and take the ball off the wires. You and your partner have the net and the offense. On the other hand let's assume your lob is just an average one, and I hit the overhead and retain control of the net. The next time I serve to you, however, you can bet your sneakers that I will be wondering whether you are going to hit the low one down the middle or lob over my head. Unfortunately I underestimate your deceptive abilities. Your next return, as I don't crowd the middle as much as I did earlier, is a short, sharply angled cross court that I watch go by, land fairly in the alley, and fall dead against the screen for a winner. Now I am really confused. I fault!

Meanwhile my net-playing partner has been sleeping as a result of inactivity on the return of serve. Watching the game develop as I leave the middle of the court to now protect against your cross-court, he has obliged by leaving his alley to cover your low returns down the middle. Sensing my net man needs to be waked — perhaps rudely — you drill my next serve down his alley for a clean winner. On the following serve my net man comes in close to the net protecting his alley, and with what do you welcome him? No, not a low shot down the middle (although that is a good alternative), but a lob over his head that lands just beyond our service line. My net man (who may not be my net man for too much longer!) is caught leaning toward the net with "glue on his sneakers" — hence, your point on a fairly ineffective shot. Next time he does not know whether to be prepared for a shot down the middle, down the alley, or a lob. By your change-of-pace shots and varied returns you have transformed a well-oiled team into a duo of mental misfits.

When nothing seems to work right, if you find yourself playing horribly while your opponents are making impossible shots (obviously playing over their heads!), slow it down. Be content to sit back and lob, lob, lob. In other words, this is the exception to the rule. Be overly patient in this instance, and don't take advantage of an opportunity for a while. This strategy may throw your opponents' timing off and give you a chance to regain your composure. No guarantee, but the way things were going it might have been a short, rather embarrassing match anyway.

In the quarter-finals of the Rye tournament a few years ago, Kim

Kimberly and I played Dick Squires and Doug Russell. Frankly, the match went so fast we were not sure whether we had played in it or not! I think we got nine points and one game in two sets! I was only thankful it was not a best-of-five-sets match. They played extremely well and we were terrible — probably because they made us play poorly. This is a bad example of being overly patient; we never tried it, but we should have. We just didn't have time to think of it. We were swept off the court before we could change our game plan. Don't think as slowly as we did that day. If you and your partner find yourselves in one of these nightmarish predicaments, try the lowly lob over and over again.

Here are a few tactics — some serious and some not so serious. Remember, if nothing else works, there are ways to win anyway if you are a devotee of Vince Lombardi's "Winning isn't the only thing; it is everything!"

1. If you play against a team with one good player and one not so good player, try playing the not so good player exclusively. First, you will tire him out; second, you will send the good player "around the bend and up the wall." Give the good player an *occasional* shot and he will blow it. He is so frustrated he will very likely attempt a winning shot when the opportunity is not there. Under these pressures the not so good player will tend to be overly defensive — he will not take advantage of an opportunity.

2. Early in the morning you may run up against an opponent who had a terrific time the night before, or he might be the type who just doesn't get started before noon — play him! Even give him setups. If you find he misses them, give him some more until you get him completely discouraged and distraught. You might even kid him that you have never seen him play as well as this before. Perhaps you will lose a friend, but your chances of winning the match are greatly enhanced.

3. Drop shot on a cold day — particularly if you are playing against a pleasantly plump, glue-footed opponent. This might result in a cold stare, but, again, winning is the only thing.

4. When you spin your paddle to decide who will serve and who will have the choice of courts at the beginning of a match, sometimes surprise your opponents and give them the serve. Initially this might shake them up a bit, and if by some stroke of luck you can break ser-

vice, you are well on your way to having the match in your hip pocket. At least the momentum will be with you at the outset. As a matter of fact, some of the better teams usually elect to receive if they win the toss. The theory is that the first-time server will be a little cold and/or "clutched" (tense).

5. If you are playing a three-out-of-five-set match, you are entitled to a break after three sets. If you feel your opponents have the momentum, take the break. If momentum is not a factor but you are out of shape compared to your younger opponents, again, take the break. If the reverse is the case, however, stay on the court and "assume" everyone's ready to commence the fourth set.

6. If nothing else works, after a very close line call on the opponents' side of the court, offer to call the lines on *both* sides. If they are serving, ask the server if he minds if you keep your eye on his foot to make sure he does not foot fault. Or, better yet, ask him if he has always had that funny "hitch" in his service motion. These tactics might be dubbed "dirty paddle" and I don't condone them during a serious match, but they are known to work occasionally, and normally they do not result in bodily harm to anyone!

In conclusion, although I have great respect for the late Vince Lombardi, winning is *not* everything. Have fun and certainly try to do your very best. Paddle is a great game involving wonderful people. I cannot count the number of friends and good acquaintances I have made playing platform tennis over the years. Although I am no longer a factor in National competition, I still enjoy playing and seeing familiar faces and a few new ones as they come along. Paddlers, for the most part, are fine sportsmen. They will bend over backward to give their opponents a fair shake, and it is a tremendous feeling to be playing competitively against such people.

I owe an awful lot to the game and the people I have played with and against. I plan to continue playing both in competition and just for fun as long as I physically can. I hope that some day one of my sons may have the good fortune of winning the National Men's Doubles diadem. Perhaps by then he will be competing for $50,000 in first-prize money rather than just a silver or pewter mug. I am not so sure that is progress, but it is probably inevitable as the sport is given greater exposure and becomes more popular and widely played.

Peggy Stanton, teamed with the legendary Charlotte Lee, won the National Women's crown for four consecutive years, 1967–1970. Usually facing younger opponents, Charlotte and Peggy lost only *one set* during their four-year reign. In 1967, in six rounds of competitive play, they lost only nine games on their way to the U.S. title. Peggy was a finalist in the National Mixed (with William C. Breed III in 1969), and in 1974 she and Oden Cox won the National Senior Women's (50 and over). An outstanding tennis player as well, she has held National and high Eastern rankings in the Senior Women's Doubles. Also, she's a good golfer, skier, and swimmer. Peggy is now very much involved with the administration of paddle and is currently the only woman on the American Platform Tennis Association's Board of Directors.

15. | PEGGY STANTON

Winning Strategy in Women's Doubles

"LINESMEN READY? Players ready? Play!"

You grip the paddle tightly — so tightly that it becomes a part of your hand. Keep your eye on the ball and only the ball. Keep telling yourself, "Watch the ball." Tune out the distractions, the noise, people moving around the outside of the court, dogs barking, the sun, the icy drizzle, the wind, etc. The ball is in play. Be patient. Shots are exchanged. A brief flurry ensues. You command the net. The opponents' lobs are coming back — high — real backbreakers. You and your partner try to hit the balls into the corners softly, so they will die gently on the wires. You both also keep probing the middle, hitting easy overheads and volleys to the back wire between your opponents. Perhaps they will hesitate as to who takes the shot and who make an error. Here's the opening! The ball is coming in low and short over the net. Cut it off with a drop shot. The ball dies and rolls into the side boards. A winner and a crucial point for your team! The umpire sits alertly in his chair, bundled to the eyes in everybody's coats and blankets. The temperature hovers around twenty degrees. What a scene! What fun!

Platform tennis, though an easier game to play than tennis, still requires practice and the development of skills in order to excel. You try to perfect your shots, working into a rhythm so they flow easily at your command. When you are serving, serve deeply to your opponent's less strong side — usually her backhand. As you have only one serve, you must not make an error. Mix up your serves occasionally and keep the opposition guessing. Your partner must always be ready to protect her alley or return a lob.

The lob is not only a defensive weapon but a very effective offensive tactic as well. If your lob on the return of serve is deep enough you and your partner may take the net. Defensively, the lob is frequently used when returning balls off the wires. Occasionally, however, you can hit a smash off the side or a drive off the back wires. You must wait for just the right moment before trying to execute a forcing shot, but when the opportunity presents itself, go for it! You will have the element of surprise working to your advantage.

In practicing all these shots, you have to keep a firm wrist — especially on the volley. Often the server is in a better position than her partner at the net to cover the volley down the middle. But if you and your teammate have worked out a strategy whereby you (at net) can cut off the return, by all means do it.

One of the best shots for women's play is the drop volley. When your partner is serving, and you are at the net and the ball is returned cross court, poach and drop the ball at an angle to the side wire. If the ball is returned straight at you, block it. In colder weather the ball may drop just over the net as in a well-executed stop volley. A deep drop volley, or one with a high bounce, will enable your opponents to assume the offense. For myself, I have found that cutting off the ball with a drop volley whenever possible on my opponent's return of serve or in play is one of my most effective shots, but it does have to be made very delicately and deftly or you could be in real trouble!

As a match lengthens you may have to call on reserves of strength and stamina, so any shot that shortens play is highly desirable. Women only need power in certain situations, such as in cracking a good drive or in hitting overheads so they go into the deep screens. But they always need to hit the ball *firmly*. The emphasis is on placing the ball well, however, with soft shots to the back wire, to the corners, and to the side wires.

When you and your partner are playing a match, it is extremely important not to make outright errors when serving and returning serve. From the right court take the ball on your forehand as often as possible. Position your body to meet the ball on the rise and blast it past the opponent at net on her backhand side or aim your drive cross court to the incoming server's alley. If everything is going well, and your returns are working, hit away. If not, play it safe and lob or hit for the middle of the court.

From the left side of the court, the drive on the return of serve can be a blistering attack with a devastating cross-court shot or a deceptive drive down the net woman's alley. You have to consider your options and your opponents' defenses. If you find you are successfully lobbing the opposition away from the net, pursue that course. And employ as many low-risk returns as possible. It stands to reason that the team making the least errors will win.

When you do get the chance for a putaway shot, do not overhit it. Temper your shot so it becomes a winner. You have to play the percentages in platform tennis, which requires prolonged patience and enormous concentration. You have to have the ability to make your opportunities pay off. I find that mentally keeping the score in a match and riveting my eyes on the ball improve my concentration. Concentrating on the ball is one of the hardest things to do, especially when you are being hustled and the tempo of the game is increasing.

When you have played many times with the same partner, you will find that without even looking you will know where she is on the court. You will sense each other's presence and positions. You will then be moving together as a team. Both players will be ready for the next shot. Teamwork quickens anticipation. There are many combinations that make good partners. One player may be the steady one, always returning shots and concentrating on keeping the ball in play. The other partner may be the shot maker, taking advantage of her teammate's setups. A good team is usually composed of two players whose styles complement one another and whose personalities blend. There should be a strong rapport or "chemistry" between partners. It is essential you both share the same viewpoint about platform tennis and how you should go about winning. Lacking this compatibility when the chips are down, you are going to be in deep trouble. As a match progresses you must be able to help and support each other. If one is making a large number of errors, the other partner will have to play doubly hard until momentum is regained. A few words of encouragement can work wonders.

There are many elements that go into the making of a champion and the winning strategy to become one. Foremost, I think, is the intense *desire* to do your very best. All champions are motivated toward excellence of performance, in which they take great pride. To win a tournament at the top of one's game is most rewarding and satisfying. One of the biggest factors in any triumph is confidence. *Confidence* with a capital C. Not only must you be confident in yourself, but you must also have confidence in your partner's abilities. You know that no matter how things turn out you both have tried 100 percent. With this important and essential feeling of confidence comes *communication*. As you are both warming up on the court, you should be sizing up your opponents' strengths and weaknesses. Talk to your partner and put your game plan into action. You may find that it may have to be revised if the particular strategy is not working, so be alert and switch tactics if necessary. In play, you must both communicate, saying "Yours" or "Mine" so you won't be trapped into that awkward situation of the ball landing between you for a point.

The following comments are really directed to the aspiring tournament player rather than the just-for-fun-play-with-the-husband-or-kids-on-weekends type of paddle distaffer. There will be moments when you are behind in a fiercely competitive contest and fighting uphill, but you should never lose sight of the fact that yours is a team effort and together you are quite capable of pulling off a victory. Being "up" requires a steellike *determination to win*. It's a feeling you get in the pit of your stomach. Such determination is hardest to maintain during a long string of championship tournaments as it takes the nerves of a mountain goat, but if you care enough about winning you will sustain that desire. Being *psyched up* is very much a part of competitive platform tennis. It is a supremely positive feeling that you as a team must share. Don't ever forget that the pressure of winning is tremendous, and this pressure can only be overcome with sheer desire and confidence.

To want to win, however, is not enough. You must be physically conditioned to play as many as twelve sets in one day; i.e., four three-set matches in a tournament's first day. That's a lot of paddle! Your mental endurance has to be equally strong. Never think of the errors you have made on crucial points and easy setups. Concentrate on the point at hand. *Play each point.* "A point at a time" my partner and I will say to each other. This mental approach is especially useful when the match is very tight and a point here or there will make the difference between winning or losing. All your efforts are galvanized into each individual rally. A platform tennis match can have an uncanny resemblance to a runaway horse. The speed and tempo of the contest can be changed in a blink of the eye, and you will have all you can do just to hang in there. More matches are won by sheer determination and the intestinal fortitude never to give up. Couple that attitude with skill and some lucky breaks and you have a winning combination.

Players talk of other players having "the killer instinct." If you are going to play aggressive paddle, you must be capable of making forcing shots — and at the precise moment when a winner is desperately needed. This instinct or ability is as much a part of some competitive players as is their paddle. Other players lack it entirely. Competition brings out the best assets in many players. They thrive on matching wits, on stretching themselves up to and sometimes beyond their potential, and above all they desire to give the very best account of themselves. The main difference between a champion and an also-ran is frequently the burning desire to excel and to raise one's game when needed.

The most fun way and really the best way to improve your game is to play with men. Mixed doubles will sharpen and quicken your reflexes. As most men hit the ball harder, thereby creating longer rallies, your screen play has to improve. Most mixed doubles games contain a good deal of screen play. Your timing as you dig balls out of the corners will profit enormously. Men can hit very hard shots that bounce a long way off the wires. With practice you will be able to follow the ball and hit down on it for an offensive return. In the longer rallies you learn to be patient and try to maneuver your opposition into making an error.

Weather is a tremendous factor in platform tennis. It directly affects the ball, which in turn has an effect on your play. In the colder temperatures the ball won't bounce as high and you have to vary your strokes accordingly. A drop volley with a firm, hard ball is a certain

Up at net, poised and ready.

winner. Deep volleys to the base line are much harder to get. You can really crack the return of serve without worrying that it will take off. When the ball dies in the wires, it dies! On very warm days the ball is much livelier. Wire play is more prevalent and lengthy rallies occur. The ball bounces much higher and, therefore, is much harder to put away. At net you will be less liable to hit fliers if you keep your hands and paddle just above the net.

When you mention the weather you immediately think of clothing. It is very important to be able to move freely. You often see some (unknowing) player in a heavy jacket all bundled up like a teddy bear — completely unable to swing and move her arms. You want to be comfortable and your clothes should fit you loosely. There are, of course, the chic ladies who prefer the sleek look with mysterious dark glasses. And there are the look-alikes, fresh from the ladies' drill team, color coordinated and all. The most fun are the hats. Brimmed, trimmed, knitted, tied under the chin in yards of chiffon and worn with great flair becoming the distinctive trademark of the wearer. That's the imaginative, colorful, and informal side of women's platform tennis.

Champion platform tennis players, both men and women, make few errors, are skillful racquet-wielders, and have good control, concentration, and great versatility. They hold up well under pressure and they're fighters. All these attributes are developed (they don't just happen!) over a period of years and a good deal of hard work. They've probably lost more games than they have won, but they learned valuable lessons from their defeats. Experience gained from tournament play creates seasoned players, and losses often teach them more than victories.

Women's doubles played competitively is a stupendous *team* effort. Winning is going to take both members of the duo. Good luck to all of you who love (or will grow to love) this grand and glorious game of platform tennis. Whether you are a current champion or an aspiring challenger, play hard, play to win, but, above all, play to have fun!

Gloria Dillenbeck, a former National Senior Women's Doubles Tennis Champion (1968 with Betty Pratt) and for many years nationally ranked in singles, says that as much as she still loves tennis she actually *prefers* playing platform tennis. It's more "fun and giggles." Teamed with another New Jerseyite, B. J. DeBree, they "laughed" their way to three consecutive U.S. Women's Doubles titles — 1971, 1972, and 1973. In 1969 Gloria and Bobbie Kauffman were runners-up. In 1974 Gloria and John Mangan reached the finals of the National Mixed. For the past six years she's been conducting a Junior development program in New Jersey and twice a month instructs as many as sixty children. Off the court she's active in the theater and spends time with creative writing.

16. | GLORIA DILLENBECK

The Woman's Role in Championship Mixed Doubles

THIS CHAPTER is addressed with love, compassion, and empathy to all ladies everywhere who struggle valiantly on evenings and weekends to convince the male populace that they really *are* valuable allies on the paddle court.

Tournament-level mixed doubles have been called many things (not all complimentary, or repeatable!), but I think of them affectionately as "the masochistic woman's delight." The reason for this label is startlingly clear. In mixed doubles, the woman is invariably "played to death." Therefore, those women who compete in top-flight mixed platform tennis matches are a hardy lot with great stamina and powers of concentration. I have felt, while lobbing back the sixteenth straight tricky wire shot (in one point of a long third set), that all time had ceased and I was floating in limbo — unaware of anything except the terrible need to return the ball "one more time." So ladies, if you want to improve your wire play, I wholeheartedly recommend mixed doubles with strong men players (if they'll have you, but that's another story). You may approach physical collapse, but your entire game will certainly improve!

Tournament mixed doubles embody the general strategy of regular doubles with a few differences. As in all doubles, whoever controls the net controls the point, and a team must always strive to break serve. Like all doubles, the game of mixed is also played in and through the mind. Every point is played like a chess match. You as a team try to move your opponents around like chess pieces, attempting to maneuver them out of position and make a winning shot. This assumes a game plan of playing to their weaknesses. It also assumes *patience* — which is probably the fundamental quality in platform tennis. The other function the mind must perform is *concentration*. In any game between two evenly matched teams, the winning team will have concentrated harder and longer. The momentum of a team, which is often overwhelming in platform tennis, can only be maintained if concentration is intent and continuous. We've all witnessed matches where one team has suddenly gone "out to lunch" — and that's the end for it. Staying on top of the game mentally in a long match will inevitably be tougher on you ladies, because you will tire from being played continually.

Another characteristic of all doubles that applies to mixed is the movement of the team in tandem. You must move up together, back together, and side-to-side together. One difference here, however, is that the man will cover more of the court than you will and move in to handle short shots while you stay back to retrieve those that get past him. Of course, any man who attempts to cover too much of his partner's court is inviting trouble. If he plays her side too often, the opposition can make a point by hitting soft shots into his corner. He may get back to a few, but eventually you'll catch him — and meanwhile he'll get awfully tired.

There are three primary differences in strategy between regular and mixed doubles that affect you, the woman player. The first is that in mixed you will invariably play the forehand court, no matter which side you may be accustomed to in women's doubles. There have been cases where left-handed women tried the backhand side, but these teams have never been very successful. The second is the point that I stressed in the opening paragraphs — play your female opponent. Instead of "playing the ball" (or the shot you might normally hit), you should hit the ball to the opposing female as often as possible. Thus, three shots that are far more effective in mixed are the drop shot to the woman, the lob over her head, and the return of serve hit hard at the woman at net. The third difference between regular and mixed doubles is that your role in mixed is primarily to be consistent and make as few errors as possible. Your consistency will allow your partner to play his aggressive game without having to be overly cautious. However, I must temper this generalization where tournament-level play is concerned. Many top women players are steadier if allowed to play their own sort of game. That is, they do not simply "keep the ball in play." They are far more consistent when hitting the ball with pace and authority. This does *not* mean that they try for winners all over the place — it merely means that they hit shots that are appropriate to the strategy of the point in progress.

Thus, in mixed doubles you must be ready to "pick up the pieces." And which pieces you'll pick up will depend on the type of game your partner plays. Some men stick pretty much to a routine "sides" game with occasional forays into the forehand court to hit a winner or pick up a drop shot. Others go charging around continually and will frequently cut in front of the woman player, expecting her to run quickly to the backhand base line to retrieve any shot that passes him. If the latter sort of game shatters your nerves and leaves you standing flat-footed on your own side, then for Heaven's sake, don't agree to play with that type of player.

That brings me to the last, and most important, part of this general discussion of mixed doubles; that is, picking a partner. Play only with a man to whose game you can adjust. Since the man must be the dominant player, you must adapt your usual game to complement his — so, if you can't adjust, don't play! The whole psychology of winning *together* is really based on that instinct with which you sense where and when he's going to move so that you can cover for him. This assumes real understanding and communication on the court. Inspire his protective instincts. Reassure him that his male gallantry toward your female opponent should be checked in the warming hut along with his storm coat before the match begins! That guy on the other side of the net will certainly hit the ball right at *your* teeth!

Now, let's get more specific and examine your part in a high-level mixed game, shot by shot. First, let's take the serve — probably the most frustrating, yet rewarding, shot in platform tennis. With only one chance to get the serve in the court, serving is always a real challenge, but in mixed doubles the pressure is far greater on you. If you throw in too safe a serve (the old marshmallow, which might be O.K. in ladies' doubles), the man will be able to bomb it back for a winner or forced error, yet you cannot afford to give away points by faulting either. One rule to remember is *always get the serve in play to the woman,* even if you must hit a weak serve. Never give up the service point to her. (To do so would be like walking the pitcher in baseball!) If you must fault, do so to the man by trying to hit a tougher serve to him.

The ideal lady partner has a consistent serve, with some pace and spin, which she moves around deep within the service box. If you can achieve this goal you will be' in great demand. Breaking serve is one way a team wins, and in mixed doubles, the woman's serve is usually the weak link. If you are able to hold serve consistently, "You've come a long way, baby!"

This brings me quite naturally to the second shot for discussion — the volley. No one can hold serve if he can't volley well, particularly that key volley hit coming into the net. After you've served you'll have to volley any kind of shot that is returned to you. Therefore, even though you are going to charge to the net as quickly as possible, you must be able to make strong volleys from midcourt. Remember that this first "approach volley" is never meant to be a winner, even should the return of service be high. Don't take chances with this shot. Merely volley it deep (probably down the middle) and "settle in" at the net. The woman player who can volley effectively from midcourt has an added advantage in nearly any type of rally. Since the net position is the winning one, your opponents will often try to lob over your head to move you back from the net. Once they have you at midcourt, they will invariably hit soft shots, which will drop low on your side. If you can volley these shots back while recapturing your net position, your partner won't have to cover for you at the net and thereby open up his side of the court. A surprising number of ladies who are good players have never mastered the midcourt volley. They are fine when tight at the net because their volleying is primarily soft and shallow. But move them back a few feet and they cannot punch the shot over.

Of course, when your partner is serving, the soft volley can be invaluable. Your male opponent will often return a serve with the "bomb" — the ball hit directly at you at net. To play this back at all, be in tight to the net so that *any* blocked shot will drop over — and let's face it, holding that paddle up in front of you with two hands is your only defense. Many's the day that I've stood at net, trembling in my sneakers, watching my opponent rock back and forth on the service line, as he waited, eyes steely, to slam the ball directly at me! Help! But, hang in there, honey — don't let that male chauvinist be intimidating! When you've blocked a few of his "Sunday Best," he may have second thoughts about pursuing that tactic and you'll have gone a long way toward upsetting his equilibrium (also known as "male ego")!

Your return of serve, the third shot for discussion, will be different from your partner's. There are basically three types of return that may be hit. First, you must be able to hit a hard flat or topspin drive. If your male opponent is serving and you are able to get set well for his serve, hit this shot at the woman net player. Otherwise, the drive should go down the middle. When the opposing woman is serving, the hard shot at her male partner will not be as effective. However, hit it occasionally, as it's a good way to keep him from poaching too often. Usually the drive return will pay off best when hit at the opposing woman server. She will have far greater trouble volleying this "heavy" shot from midcourt than will her male partner. Leave the blitzing to your partner. In mixed doubles that's his department. You should be ready to cover for him should the ball get beyond his reach.

The second type of return of serve you'll hit is the lob. When the man is serving, hit the lob over the lady at net. Either she will have to move back or the man will have to drop back and cover it for her. Regardless of who plays the shot, you will have opened up the court for your next strategem (we hope, to move in toward the net).

If your female opponent is the type of player who charges madly to the net on serve, you can occasionally catch her off balance by lobbing the return cross court over her head. This will make her more tentative coming in behind her serve, and she may then be trapped in midcourt with the third type of service return, the "change-up" or "dink." This is simply a change-of-pace shot that is hit softly cross court to die at the feet of the onrushing server. This shot, too, is more rewarding when the woman is serving, since she is usually slower afoot.

The ideal is to be able to hit all these returns of serve and not get locked into any one type. I have seen far too many players (both male and female) who, like programmed automatons, repeat the same shot over and over again, even when it is no longer effective. Remember that to break serve, you must keep your opponents off balance, and hitting a variety of returns will help to achieve this. Most important of all, however, is *get the ball in play* on the return of serve. This is especially true when you have a "break point," i.e., 15-40, with your opponent serving to you in the forehand court. In this situation, you should hit whichever return you play best, at a safe speed, and pray that sometime during the point your opponents will make an error.

The next shot in mixed doubles to consider is the overhead. Blessed is the woman with a strong overhead, for she shall hit into the corners for a "nick" (unreturnable wire shot). If you are tall or usually jump (as I do, at 5′3″ in my high-heeled sneakers) and can cover your own lobs, you will be a boon in mixed play. Your partner won't have to exhaust himself covering most of the lobs and opening up his side of the court in the bargain. If your overhead is weak, you simply must work to improve it, for virtually all of the top women players have strong overheads.

Gloria Dillenbeck is in good position for her overhead. Slight of build and rather short, she gets an unusual amount of power behind her shots. Her hitting arm is fully extended and she's left the playing deck in order to attain maximum height for her shot. She's perfectly positioned to hit the ball well in front of her body.

The last shot for discussion is the wire shot. The woman may expect to be played constantly, particularly off the wires. So woe betide the lady who is not a really grooved wire player — and there is simply *no* way to achieve this other than *constant practice*. The longer you can hit that ball back high off the wire, the better are your chances to gain an error. Always try to hit your wire lob over the woman, if possible, down her alley. The man won't be able to cover for her there and you may catch her midcourt. At any rate, make her hit most of the overheads. If nothing else, she will get tired. While most wire returns by you should be defensive, in top-level platform tennis, there are women who hit the aggressive wire shot. This return is hit somewhat flat or with topspin as the ball comes off the wires. It sails low over the net and may catch the opposing team off guard. As in any attack, the element of surprise will be lost should the same shot be used too often. Thus, this shot is most effective after you have hit a long series of typical lob returns and only if the ball rebounds off the wires just right.

My closing note is one of deep commiseration with all you ladies who habitually play the backhand side of the court in women's doubles (as do I). In mixed play you will be moved to the forehand court, which is, undeniably, a most foreign land. You must successfully face two challenges: returning serve at a different angle and playing the wires in reverse. Few people fully appreciate how terribly difficult it is to play tournament-caliber platform tennis on an unfamiliar side of the court. The return of serve must be hit earlier and with slightly more topspin, and you must be prepared to hit more lob returns off your forehand stroke than you would in the backhand court. As for the reverse wire play, you will be hitting most wire shots on your forehand rather than your backhand. The timing is different and it takes a great deal of practice to make yourself turn into the right wire as quickly as you've been grooved to turn to the left. Just be sure to allow yourself enough practice time in that right court to adjust before a mixed doubles tournament.

So, ladies, get on the courts with the men. Playing mixed is the quickest way to improve your game — and it's more fun anyhow. Never forget that while "he" is making all those flashy shots, "you" will be supplying the glue that keeps the team in the game together (ah, life in miniature!). Good luck and on to victory!

John C. Beck celebrated his forty-second birthday on March 10, 1974,
by giving himself the greatest present of all — the National Men's
Doubles platform tennis title! He and Herb FitzGibbon, playing very
aggressive and confident paddle, won the title they had been seeking
for five years. John is a second-generation member of America's most
renowned platform tennis family. His parents won the National Mixed
Doubles, and his mother annexed National titles numerous times between
1938 and 1960 in both Mixed Doubles and Women's. His sister Sue
carried on in the Beck tradition by taking the Women's crown in 1960
(with her mother) and again in 1962 and 1965. John joined the act
by teaming with his sister to win the Mixed Doubles title in 1972. John
is a left-hander and was one of the first southpaws to change over to
the deuce side of the court. What he lacks in speed he more than
compensates for with aggressive returns, a fine tournament temperament,
height (he and Herb are both 6′ 5″), and a most effective "sneaky"
drop volley.

17. | JOHN C. BECK

The Man's Role in Championship Mixed Doubles

TEAM BALANCE is important to success in any team sport — particularly racquet doubles games. It is *the* vital ingredient to success in platform tennis doubles. The presence of the screen makes for much longer rallies than in almost any other racquet sport, hence, more numerous opportunities to probe and test and to be probed and tested. Team imbalances are easily detected and quickly exploited. The weaker partner of a team invites attack. The stronger partner must, consequently, seek to alter his style of play and strategical outlook to minimize the weaker player's exposure and vulnerability to attack.

In mixed doubles the male's primary responsibility is balancing his team both on offense and defense. He starts by assessing the strengths and weaknesses of his partner, her serve, her overhead, her volley, her return of serve, her work off the wires, and her speed. He should likewise assess his own abilities. His self-appraisal is quite naturally an ego-challenging, hence, difficult, task to perform objectively. The male is best advised to discuss with his partner as many of his judgments as good taste and politics permit. He should seek her comments and criticisms so that they both agree on the tactics they'll use for optimum effectiveness. Failure to reach a mutual understanding in this regard can, and most often does, result in lack of team coordination, compatibility, and, ultimately, good will. Without the latter, all

Exciting mixed doubles play. Notice that each player concentrates on the ball.

doubles are trouble and mixed doubles, putting it mildly, are not fun.

To achieve team balance in all facets of the game requires, of course, that weaknesses in one partner be compensated for by the strengths of the other. If neither partner can serve, neither balance nor victory will ever be achieved. If neither can effectively cope with a well-placed lob, taking and holding the net on serve will prove to be impossible. While weaknesses in one partner are unlikely to be matched perfectly with offsetting, compensating strengths in the other, relative strengths can and should be used to cover relative weaknesses.

While the theory of the "weaker sex" has been proven invalid beyond any shadow of a doubt (especially on a platform tennis court!), it is still well to have the male assume as much of the physical burden of team play as he can. Unless his partner's serve is distinctly superior to his, he should always serve first. The server expends more energy than the player at net. He who serves first often serves more games in a match than his partner. He never serves fewer.

The male should serve to both opponents in such a way as to minimize their counterattack on his distaff partner at net. Ideally, his serve should force his opponents into a lob return. In a close championship match, the male should not (nor is he expected to) ease off when serving to his female opponent. His opposing counterpart won't! The defense against the lob should similarly be structured to help the female partner in her most effective fashion. Certainly she can ably handle short lobs without relinquishing her control of the net position. Medium and deep lobs, on the other hand, are probably best handled by the male. Such a strategy will minimize the pressure on your partner to recapture, as she must, her net position. Furthermore, lob returns are the most physically demanding of paddle shots. Whenever possible, the male should make the return to preserve overall team stamina. The male runs a risk in returning those medium or deep lobs thrown up over the head of his partner. If the lob is hit close to the sideline, he must pull well out of his half of the court to execute the return. Whenever he feels that he will be unable to return to his side of the court in proper time and position, he should "command" his partner (in suitable but firm fashion) to switch to his side of the court. Following his return of the lob, he will then return to his new net position in the most expeditious manner possible. His partner cannot merely stand in one position on a platform tennis court. There will be times when she will have to cover for her partner, who is constantly covering for her.

In contrast to men's doubles, where both partners can assume similar positions relative to the net, in mixed doubles it is advisable for the male to stand somewhat further back from the net than his female partner and somewhat closer to the center court line. While such a position exposes him to the challenges of both soft flat returns and hard-driven shots down his alley, this team strategy and physical balance should be more effective over the life of the match. In other words, the male has to take certain chances in mixed doubles in order to help his female partner as much as possible.

The distaff partner's serve is the most challenging and critical situation faced by the male in mixed doubles. To win a team must generally be able to "hold" its serves with regularity. Here, too, when the female is serving, the male should stand somewhat further back from the net than he ordinarily does in men's doubles and should position himself slightly closer to the center of the court. In short, he should attempt to cut off and protect as much of his and his partner's side of the court as he can — and especially to try to handle the hard-driven balls that often intimidate his partner. He should attempt to draw the return of serve to himself. Simultaneously, he must be prepared to protect his net-rushing partner from the medium or deep lob. By moving around and poaching frequently he can do much to worry and harass the opposition, particularly the female across the net, who probably is not accustomed to such aggressive play. His role, in summary, is to both intimidate and distract the opponents as well as to do everything conceivable to help his partner win her serve.

There are two distinct and contrasting defensive strategies for winning in platform tennis. One, a passive approach, is based on the theory that most games are won as a result of opponents' errors. This strategy stresses patience and "keeping the ball in play." The second style, more popular in men's doubles than mixed doubles, embodies attacking as well as strong, defensive tactics. Proper mixed doubles strategy is probably a blend of the two. The female, most often playing the forehand side of the court, returns serve rather steadily and works the ball off the wires; she is primarily concerned with keeping the ball in play and reducing her number of errors to a minimum. Her function is to try to wear down the opponents and win by attrition. Her male partner, playing the backhand court, aggressively attempts to return the serve — preferably to the female opponent for a winner. He is constantly trying to *force* an error while his distaff cohort plays the waiting game.

The severity of his shots against the opposing female should be governed in largest measure by her level of skill. In simple terms, the shot should be hit hard enough to produce a winner or at least to make her a little wary, but never so hard as to do her any bodily harm. Against the highly skilled female, this is a difficult and fine line to draw. Common sense must unequivocally override your burning desire to win. After all, it *is* only a game!

A short note on court sides. The usual practice is for the male to play the backhand court because he *can* be more aggressive from that side. There is more court, and there are greater angles to shoot for. In addition, more important, critical points occur in the left court (ad in or ad out). Even in men's doubles, the right-court, or forehand player is more often the steady one, always trying to set up his partner. So it follows that the female will be more at home in the forehand court and more helpful with her steady style of play.

The defensive male's role, once the serve has been returned, is as obvious as the offensive strategy used against his team. His female partner is likely to be the focus of the opponents' attention and attack. The male must attempt to maintain as much team balance as circumstances permit. He should employ tactics that draw shots to himself and retrieve short shots into his partner's front court. From this position he may also attempt to intercept mis-hit or short overhead returns of his partner's deeper lobs. In this manner he equalizes to the extent possible the offensive pressures that typically are brought to bear on his partner.

In general, platform tennis mixed doubles can be, and usually are, more fun than tennis mixed doubles. The female can much more effectively hold up her half of the court, and the male can also really do something to help her out. The court is much smaller than a tennis court, and this provides the male with many more opportunities to cover, to intercept, to harass the opponents.

Mixed doubles can be every bit as enjoyable and as challenging as men's doubles. Good team balance is critical, and the male's primary role is that of the balancer. He must be physically and mentally prepared to back up and support his female partner on any and every rally. If he is not, he will quickly discover by the play of the male opponent across the net that there is no place for gallantry on a platform tennis court.

Edward M. Prince is one of the few players outside the
northeastern area to advance to the semifinals of the National Men's
Doubles (1972). Paired with former National Junior Tennis champion
Ted Rogers, also from Chevy Chase, Maryland, they won the first
Middle Atlantic tournament the same year. In 1971 and 1973 Ted
pulled Dick Squires to victories in the Western Pennsylvania Men's
Invitational. A patent lawyer in Washington, D.C., Ted is also an
excellent tennis player and has been a runner-up three times in his club's
golf championship. He's the perfect author on the subject of steadiness
as he has the reputation of being "Paddle's Prince of Patience" or
"Steady Teddy." His outstanding offensive stroke is a low, hard return
of serve from the ad court — which he hits, needless to say, with a high
degree of consistency.

18. | EDWARD M. PRINCE

The Art of Steadiness

DON'T MAKE ERRORS. This is the beginning, the middle, and the end of the concept of steadiness. Steadiness is not dramatic; it lacks color and glamour. But it is in this area that the game of platform tennis presents its greatest challenge and offers, in turn, its greatest rewards.

The sport of platform tennis, even when played by the finest competitors, is probably 90 percent *errors*. These errors fall into two categories — careless errors and forced errors. There is only one type of careless error, and that type is simply a very bad shot. Forced errors, on the other hand, comprise two categories that may be briefly described as those which are causally related to your opponent's good shot and those which are causally related to your own careless shot. I'm particularly concerned with careless errors and careless shots leading to forced errors and needlessly lost points.

Despite all that can be written on the importance of steadiness, the game will always consist of 90 percent of the points being decided by errors rather than by winning shots. This rather pessimistic remark is not unexpected because of the small size of the court and the fact that two people are covering this relatively limited area. Steadiness hopefully will result in fewer errors being charged to your team than your opponent's team.

Like all shots in the game of platform tennis, steadiness is, indeed, an art. It is a concept easily understood, yet one of the most difficult concepts to teach or to master. There is always that great temptation to smash the ball as hard as you can. *Steadiness* can be defined as the *art of playing within one's ability with a minimum of errors.* Inasmuch as the abilities of players will vary greatly, the concept of steadiness calls for a certain adaptation in each individual's game.

The importance of steadiness should not be underestimated. A good player is often judged by the consistency with which he hits hard forcing shots. In other words, what his "batting average" is. A distinction is drawn between steadiness and consistency in hitting hard shots, although the distinction is somewhat subtle. While the concepts may be different, they are very much interrelated. Every good player who has a forcing shot of high consistency also has the capacity to play with steadiness or within his capabilities. Patience and steadiness enable the good player to wait for the opportunity to hit the forcing shots that, in turn, lead to higher consistency and percentages of success for such shots. Individually, therefore, steadiness is important in that you *wait* for the good forcing shot.

The game of platform tennis is made up of team personalities, each possessing dual components of varying steadiness, speed, patience, reflexes, strength, and all of the other traits that determine a player's total ability. It goes without saying that a team can only be as steady or as strong as its weakest link. Each member of the team has particular strengths and weaknesses. Steadiness, therefore, in a good team is absolutely essential in order to protect the weaknesses of each member of the team while, at the same time, setting up shots for the strengths of each teammate. If one player has an especially strong offensive game, the other player should complement him with steadiness and by setting up his partner's strength through such steadiness.

Aside from improving individual consistency by waiting for better shots and complementing your partner's strengths, steadiness has another important function. If you are having an off day and cannot seem to get your own forcing shots going well, a resort to steadiness may very well revive your game. Then too, a set can slip away very quickly. By resorting to steadiness — the "waiting game" — you are in a better position to buy a little more court time and to try to get back into the match. In other words, make your opponent stay out on the court a long time to see whether he can continue hitting good shots and whether you will continue to experience difficulties. In many instances, you will regain your touch just as rapidly as your opponent loses his effectiveness, and the entire complexion of the game can be turned around. You must make your opponent work for his points so that you can work yourself back into the match.

A competitive match may be influenced adversely by playing conditions — the condition of the court, the screens, the weather, the ball, et al. Steadiness may be the answer to overcoming these conditions. For instance, if it is raining, it will be more difficult to control hard shots and the ball will skid (both off your paddle and the court surface), thereby making steady play more desirable. Under difficult playing conditions, such as a wet court, spongy, soggy ball, or cold weather, the net player will have a great advantage. This advantage, however, can be partially overcome if errors from the backcourt are held to a minimum.

Throughout this entire discussion, it must be remembered that steadiness is only one aspect of a person's ability. Every steady player should be able to generate an offensive shot *at the right time*. By waiting for the opportune moment, the offensive shot can be relatively easy, forcing, and even devastating. Conversely, by executing a forcing shot at an inopportune moment, the possibility of making a "stupid" error is greatly enhanced.

If steadiness is the art of playing within one's ability, it must necessarily be a product of the most basic fundamentals in any racquet sport, namely, watching the ball and using good judgment. Judgment, of course, is critical as to the type of shot you hit and where and when you hit it. If you watch the ball and hit good, purposeful shots, you will develop a rhythm that, particularly on defense, is essential to steadiness. This rhythm may frustrate your opponent to a point where he attempts a low percentage shot beyond his capability. At the same time, rhythm will enable you to develop patience and consistency in your shots and strategy.

If you think that steadiness means sending up a myriad of soft lobs, hitting nothing but the easy and obvious shots, and merely playing "poop ball paddle" until you eventually lose the point, it is easy to understand why you might conclude that steadiness is no fun or not for you. A steady player does not have to be one who simply postpones the inevitable, i.e., that fatal error. To the contrary, he can make the inevitable happen; he can control the tempo of the game, forcing his opponent into situations in which the opponent is uncomfortable, extended, or, it is to be hoped, thoroughly frustrated and "going out of his mind." Steadiness can be a great mental challenge because it gives the steady player control of the game. It can also be very taxing on patience. Most importantly, steadiness can be just as offensively oriented as any other aspect of the game.

The theory of offensive steadiness is to force your opponent into errors with *low-risk shots*. These shots are not ones that will make a dramatic change in the outcome of a particular point, such as forcing shots. Rather, offensive steadiness is the concept of making shots that *could* force your opponent into errors *if* he is careless. Patience is an absolute requirement since many offensive shots of a steady nature will produce *no* errors. Persistence and patience will be amply rewarded if your opponent's game is not equal to your steadiness. If, however, you do not *think offensively,* you will become recognized as a strictly defensive player who cannot hurt the opposition.

Each aspect of the game has nuances with respect to the art of steadiness. These variations are more apparent in backcourt play than in forecourt play. With respect to the serve, it is axiomatic that steadiness is manifested in the lack of faults. An easy serve is certainly more reliable and steadier than a hard serve. By moving the ball around the service box and by aiming the ball at your opponent's weakness — such as his backhand — you can be a little steadier while still maintaining an offensive approach to the serve.

When volleying or hitting overheads from the net position, steadiness is exemplified by not making careless shots that result in an easy forcing shot by your opponent and by not making careless errors. The proper position at net will minimize careless shots. Steadiness in net play, however, is a combination of mental alertness and good judgment. At all times, you must be aware of your opponents' strengths. Each of your opponents, on the other hand, will have one or two shots that he does not normally turn into a forcing, offensive shot. In most situations, for instance, a shot to your opponent's backhand will be a relatively safe shot. Under these circumstances, steadiness dictates that you aim a large number of balls to the opposition's backhand while patiently waiting for a shot that goes out or that can be turned into a good offensive shot.

If your opponent has a glaring weakness, keep exploiting it while you are at the net. This weakness is a low-risk shot. It is highly un-likely that any inherent weakness will disappear during the course of the match. A temporary weakness, however, can easily be corrected over the period of two sets. Absolute patience must be exercised in exploiting the low-risk backcourt zones. Your opponent is apt to re-sort to "steady" play when the ball comes into these zones due to his inability to turn such shots into offensive, forcing shots. In the long run, therefore, the player with the greatest patience will prevail. This strategy does not mean you do not tempt your opponents' stronger shots. You should pick the proper time, however, for exploiting those zones from which offensive power shots can be executed. The proper time occurs when you have perfect net position and your opponents are slightly extended and off balance.

In other words, after frustrating your opponents with a series of low-risk shots, you may want to test their patience with a shot that is not quite to their liking but certainly is the best shot they have seen in the last ten offerings! Through a series of shot selections, you might frus-trate the opponents into making a careless error. The concept of steadiness at the net, therefore, is one of exploiting your opponents' zones of *minimum* offensive potency. Before or during a match, dis-cuss strategy with your partner so that you can both work effectively to achieve the desired result. Of equal importance is the fact that your volleys and overheads should not be forced. Do not hit a shot too hard out of frustration since it is apt to rebound from the screen so far that your opponents have an opportunity to make an offensive shot that hurts you.

Play in the backcourt is the area in which steadiness becomes most readily apparent. It starts with a return of serve, off which many win-ners and many losers are hit. If you want to maximize steadiness while sacrificing some of your offensive power, you must not try to hit every ball through or by your opponents. However, this is steadiness with-out a purpose.

The purpose of steadiness is low-risk offense — offense with a pur-pose, with reason, dedicated to the single goal of forcing your oppo-nents into erring. Most serves will bounce up to a point that is higher than the net. It is at this point that you want to hit the ball down so that it passes low over the net and reaches the server at a point well below net level — with the hope that it will result in a volleying error into the net. A relatively flat return is suggested in order to minimize the likelihood of error. The topspin forehand, when hit easily, is apt to produce more errors than a flat shot, unless you particularly concentrate on clearing the net.

The return suggested is a simple blocked shot, with the paddle head raised above the hand. The shot is hit with a very short, compact stroke, which is more of a punch shot than a fully extended swing. The paddle head is angled slightly downward so as to return the ball on a line designed to pass over the top of the net and then land below the net level to the point of the volley return. You should be moving forward, knees bent so as to get your eyes closer to the ball. If the ball is served into your body or has an unusual amount of spin, it may be desirable to hit a little cut shot. This shot is made by moving the paddle on a downward and forward extending path with a slightly "open" paddle face.

Still another type of steady, reliable service return is to catch the ball on the rise with a blocked, soft cross-court shot, a "dink," away from the reach of the opposing net man. The advantage that stems from hitting the serve early and on the rise is the fact that this move will catch the server further back from the net and will give the ball more time to drop below the level of the net.

These low shots should be mixed with lobs to keep your opponents from crowding the net on their return. While these low shots do not produce dramatic winners, they are apt to draw your opponents into careless errors. In a crucial situation, low shots keep the pressure on the server and, more importantly, avoid giving away what could be a pivotal point.

At least half the game is played in the backcourt. It is often said that it is a great advantage to have the serve and be at the net. This advantage stems principally from the fact that players are less steady in the backcourt than in the forecourt. Your reward for patience, however, is more vividly illustrated in backcourt play than in play at the net. The speed with which the ball lands in the hitting area is an important factor for improving steadiness. Thus, if you allow the speed of the ball to be reduced by permitting it to rebound off the screening, you will be in a better position to control the next shot. Low shots can be returned off the wires, with either the forehand or backhand, without trying to drive the ball through your opponents. If the opposition is caught off guard or has started to retreat for the anticipated lob, your low shot might cause them to make an error. Any time you hit a low, steady shot, though, you must be acutely aware of the positions of the net players. If they have good balance and position at the net, it is relatively easy for them to hit a drop shot winner off a low, non-forcing shot.

It goes without saying that in any circumstance *good judgment* in the type of shot to hit must be exercised. Low shots can be hit when your opponents are back from the net, even though they may be advancing toward the net, or when you are well within the base line — as in returning a service or a short shot. On all of these shots, try to be somewhat *unpredictable,* that is, hit different types of shots to different areas of your opponents' court during the course of the match. Keep them off balance and guessing. You start off with one great advantage on every low shot, and that is you know where you are going to hit the ball while your opponents do not! Don't give away that advantage by being predictable in your shot making. Nonpredictability does not mean, however, that you force the shot. It simply means that sometimes you hit the shot down the line, other times down the middle, and still other times at the spot where you last saw your opponents. If you are not in a good position to hit a low return, hit a lob and get back into good position.

The offensive lob that you purposely try to hit over the head of the opposing net man is a high-risk shot. A low risk or steady lob, on the other hand, is not one that is intended to drop over the outstretched paddle of the net man. Quite clearly, low risk means that the lob should not hit long. The most effective means for reducing the likelihood that the lob will be out is to absorb some of the force of the shot by hitting it a little higher than normally. The steady lob can also be offensively oriented. First, it can force a return overhead into a particular area of the court from which an offensive shot can be executed. For instance, a good lob down the line will often force your opponent to hit his overhead cross court where your partner is waiting with a forcing forehand. Second, a high, deep, steady lob can force the net man away from the net, thereby setting up the possibility of a low return of the overhead aimed at catching the opponent before he can get back to net. The most important thing to remember, however, is that once you get your opening (in that your opponent has backed away from the net or is off balance) do not force the next shot unless you are in an excellent position to do so.

Too often players see the opening, but, unfortunately, the return of the ball is not quite to their liking. Nevertheless, having seen the opening for a possible winner, a player will be tempted to force or rush in order to take advantage of the opportunity. It is absolutely essential you be patient and *wait* for the *right* opening — not just for any opening. If you do not have the right opening, hit a little easier controlled shot to see whether you can provoke an error. Steadiness at that stage of the point could be very beneficial. You absolutely must *believe* you will get another chance in the near future that will be just as good, if not better. If you do believe and practice this theory, you will not be in any particular rush to end the point.

By "steady" play you have a greater opportunity to think about the appropriate shot and to catch your opponent off guard at some time. For example, during the course of a rally, you may want to go down the line to the net man, hoping to catch him "asleep." When you make up your mind to go down the line, do not force the shot. If your opponent is asleep, a ball hit with moderate pace will be almost as effective as a hard shot and may have a greater percentage of success when you consider the errors that result from attempting too difficult, too forceful shots.

In all "steady" shots, *do not slap the ball.* Keep the paddle on the ball as long as you can. In other words, be as smooth and fluid as possible in your stroke production. Don't attempt shots that you can't make. Decide where to hit the ball, and don't panic if your opponents have the spot well covered. Be prepared to start over again and proceed with your overall game plan. As you watch the ball and develop a rhythm, you will begin to develop a feel of where the ball is vis-à-vis the paddle face and you will be able to hit some low shots off the wires in order to keep your opponents honest. Again, these shots do not have to be forcing shots. They are only intended to catch your opponents by surprise and possibly produce an error.

If you look at offensive steadiness as a series of low-risk shots, you might question how one ever develops proficiency in some of the higher risk shots. During informal practice sessions, you will no doubt try shots somewhat beyond your normal capabilities, hoping to accomplish a higher degree of proficiency in these more difficult shots. In practice you should be attempting to expand your repertoire of offensive shots. During these informal matches, however, there frequently occurs a moment when trying to win a specific point or game is critical (or you can pretend it is). At that point, you should be able to revise your strategy and go all out (with steadiness!) to win. If steadiness is not a challenge during practice matches, you should occasionally turn to your partner and suggest a sort of contest as to which one of you will make the fewest errors during the ensuing few games. The style of play of your team may well change by such an experiment, but you will note that in most cases new and better results will occur. Steadiness becomes all-important during a tournament match, since invariably (for all the reasons mentioned in this chapter) the team making the fewest errors will undoubtedly win. Have fun while practicing, experiment, and try new shots, but every so often pretend you and your partner *must* win the next few games — then go after them. In other words, simulate pressure so that when you are competing in a "live" match you will be more accustomed to playing under tense circumstances and moments.

In summary, steadiness is a highly individualistic component of the sport of platform tennis. It is not the only component, by any means, but a good player knows how to play with steadiness when the situation calls for it. Success in adopting steadiness as an integral component of your game is dependent upon your patience, judgment, and mental alertness. Next time on the court, *think offensively with low-risk shots* and your effectiveness as a platform tennis competitor will improve immeasurably.

Steadiness is more than just a philosophical approach to your stroke production and strategy on the court. It is a *mental attitude that disciplines* and controls your natural impulses to "crush" every ball.

By now the message must be clear. In this racquet and ball sport — perhaps more than any other — "playing the percentages" is far more important and strategically sounder than power. Patience, consistency, concentration, restraint, steadiness, purpose, and tenacity are the positive characteristics the better players exhibit. The erratic, flashy slugger "looks good," hits occasional, unbelievable outright winners — and always is eliminated in the *first* round of every tournament of any significance!

Lucie Bel McAvoy and Mig Simpson.
Lucie's instructional program is one of the main reasons why platform
tennis, especially Women's and Juniors', has exploded in Philadelphia's
Main Line area. For the last few winters, she and Mig Simpson have
devoted much time to their clinics, which started out as an altruistic
project and have now become a profitable venture. Most paddlers are
thirsting for sound coaching and, according to Lucie, there are just not
enough hours in the day to take on all the pupils desiring lessons.
Lucie and Mig's theories of strokes and strategies are sound and helped
them win the 1971 National Consolation Doubles and the 1973 Middle
Atlantic Platform Tennis Association's Women's crown. Lucie and John
Davison won the Philadelphia area Mixed Doubles title in 1974.
   Margaret Simpson, with Lucie, has been a leading light for paddle in
the Philadelphia area. In addition to her tournament wins with Lucie,
Mig and Eric Moore annexed the M.A.P.T.A. Philadelphia District
Mixed title in 1972. She recently commented, "It has been particularly
gratifying to both Lucie and me to have taught so many new players
in our ladies' clinics. This year [1973–1974] about 70 percent of the
two hundred girls we instructed were new to the game."

19. | LUCIE BEL MCAVOY & MIG SIMPSON

Conducting a Women's Platform Tennis Clinic

IN THE PHILADELPHIA AREA we have a structured program for women's clinics that has proven to be highly successful. The combination of both drills and specific playing times sustains enthusiasm while rapidly developing the skills of the players. Remember, platform tennis is a relatively easy sport to learn and, therefore, quick to enjoy only if the beginner is taught the basic fundamentals and strategy properly from the very start. The following procedures serve as our guidelines for instructing novices:

1. Four consecutive weekly sessions. It is important to schedule a fifth day in the beginning to allow for a possible rainout.
2. Sessions from 9:00 A.M. to 10:30 A.M. and 10:30 A.M. to 12 noon. (On three courts, one-and-one-half-hour playing times per foursome accommodates twenty-four players.)
3. One instructor per court.
4. Twelve balls per court.

We encourage players at the intermediate or advanced levels to sign up as foursomes.

Clinic Day I

Instructors should demonstrate each drill involved that initial day, explaining first the correct paddle grips and then the skills involved.

A. *Volley Drill:* 15 minutes

With two women in playing position at the net and two in the opposite backcourt (they will pick up balls), the instructor *throws* six consecutive balls approximately two feet over the net to the first player's forehand volley and then repeats this to the second net player. The instructor continues the drill to the players' backhand volley. Players one and two exchange positions with players three and four and the drill is repeated.

We use the volley drill first in our clinic session as we feel it sharpens the player's power of concentration and gives her an immediate feeling of accomplishment and enthusiasm. In other words, it is an easier stroke to learn — but no less important — than the ground strokes and a perfect way to introduce the players to the different "feel" of the sponge-rubber ball against the wooden paddle.

Most players often fail to:

1. Hit out in front.
2. Hit short aggressive punch shots with a firm, cocked wrist.
3. Keep elbows down when making contact with the ball.
4. Stand with weight on balls of feet and bend knees, particularly on low volleys.
5. Keep firm grips when hitting.

B. *Forehand and Backhand Ground Strokes Drill:* 20 minutes

The instructor stands at the net and throws consecutive balls to each player's forehand. She repeats drill to each player's backhand. When the players are not hitting with the instructor, they may hit against opposite court side screen.

Players most often fail to:

1. Turn sideways to net.
2. Get paddles back early.
3. Bend knees.
4. Keep wrists firm.
5. Hit backhands far enough in front and keep arms close to body.
6. Shift their weight forward when making contact with the ball.

C. *Service Drill:* 20 minutes

With players at the base line, the instructor demonstrates a correct serve and then has each player serve twelve balls into the deuce and ad courts (moving in toward the net after each service). Players not serving should be hitting services into side wires in the opposite back-court.

Most players often fail to:

1. Reach up for the ball and make contact out front with fully extended arms.
2. Keep their front foot stationary.
3. Get paddles in volleying position when running in toward the net.

D. *Playing Time:* 20-25 minutes

The instructor explains court positions and reviews the official rules. The foursome plays regulation games with latitude being given for specific rules, i.e., two services if needed for continuity of the game, etc. Instructor also analyzes individual skills.

Clinic Day II

Instructors should demonstrate how to hit overheads and wire shots (both back and corner). It is very important to explain how to anticipate the angles. Giving wire drills the second day is essential as the players *must* "think wires" as an integral and very important part of platform tennis play.

A. *Repeat Volley Drill:* 10 minutes

This is a good quick warm-up for eyeball coordination. Have each player volley both diagonally and down the line.

B. *Serve and Volley Drill:* 20-25 minutes

With women in playing position, one player serves and charges the net several times into the deuce court and the receiver returns each ball for the server to volley. Do not play an entire point. Repeat this into the ad court. Then her partner serves, which provides opponents continuity in returning service. Finish the drill with opponents serving and volleying. Encourage net player to cut off center-court returns of service.

C. *Forehand and Backhand Wire Drill:* 15-20 minutes

The instructor stands between the net and service line on the *same* side of the net as the player. The player stands in position at the base line. The instructor bounces the ball deep in the court so that it goes into the wires, and the player in waiting position at the base line returns a lob off the wires. (The lob return is encouraged in order to give the beginning player time to recover for her next shot.)

Most players often fail to:

1. Get paddles back as the ball advances toward the wires.
2. Turn sideways to net.
3. Bend knees.
4. Move in close enough to screens.

D. *Playing Time:* 20 minutes

The instructor should analyze the players' weaknesses and stop the play when necessary to show them specific skills or strategy.

E. *Lob Return of Service Drill:* 15 minutes

Women are in playing position. The first player serves three or four balls into the deuce court and her opponent lobs each return diagonally or down the center. She then serves three or four balls into the ad court. The other three players repeat the same drill.

Most players often fail to:

1. Get paddles back in time.
2. Open their paddle face and hit with a continuous swing up and out.
3. Think depth as well as height.

This is an important skill for the instructor to demonstrate at this point. She should also advise the players how to anticipate their opponents' lobs and be in position to move in with an offensive overhead.

Most players often fail to:

1. Anticipate and get back quickly enough.
2. Reach up and hit down on the ball with their arms fully extended.
3. Make contact with ball out front.
4. Aim toward opponents' back corners or down the middle.

Clinic Day III

Instructors should review and demonstrate again the wire drills. Emphasize that the player should get her paddle back and think "slow motion" while hitting the lob returns. Also explain by demonstrating the angles of the ball coming off the wires. Be sure she does not follow ball into the side wires.

A. *Repeat Forehand and Backhand Wire Drill:* 15 minutes

While the instructor is drilling one player, two other players may practice the same drill at the other end of the court. Stress the importance of a lob return off the wires. At this point the instructor should hit diagonally into the back screen so that the player can judge or anticipate the various angles. Practice and more practice is the only way to learn the angles of screen play. Advise players how to practice with their partners up at the net and hit short lobs to them.

B. *Corner Wires Drill (Side-Back):* 15 minutes

The instructor stands on the same side of net and hits diagonal overheads into side-back wires of the deuce court. The player is in position at the back screen thinking "paddle back and lob return." Remind the intermediate player that should the ball come off the wires far enough into the court area she has the option of an offensive drive. Two players may practice the drill together at the other end of the court.

Most players often fail to:

1. See Items 1, 2, and 3 under *Forehand and Backhand Wire Drill.*
2. Move into position at back wires. (Players shouldn't follow the ball into the side wires, as it will frequently come out to them.)
3. Relax and think of the wires as being friendly and helpful — not something to be feared.

C. *Playing Time:* 20-25 minutes

D. *Offensive Drive Return of Service:* 15 minutes

The instructor demonstrates and explains the need for the low, forcing cross-court return of service. With four women in playing position, one player serves two or three balls into the deuce court and the receiver practices hitting low, hard-drive returns. The server hits two or three more shots into the ad court and the second receiver repeats hard-drive return. The server's partner continues (repeats the same drill), and then the serve rotates to the other two players.

Most players often fail to:

1. Get paddles back early.
2. Hit balls soon enough.
3. Get in position to return ball with their forehand (which is usually their strongest shot).
4. Move into the ball with weight behind shots.

E. *Playing Time:* Remainder of session.

Players should be encouraged to use either type of offensive return of service — lob or drive. The server should be reminded of the importance of a deep service. Encourage the receiver to decide *early* the kind of service return she plans to hit.

Clinic Day IV

A. *Warm-up Period:* 5 minutes

B. *Overhead-Corner Wire Drill:* 20-25 minutes

Two players are in volleying position at the net and two players are in the opposite backcourt in position to return corner wire shots. The instructor stands in the center of the base line and lobs to the net players, who hit overheads diagonally into the corners. Players rotate net and back corner positions so that each has practiced all four shots.

C. *Playing Time:* 30-35 minutes

Instructor reminds the player she must "think wires" when the opponent is hitting an offensive overhead. Emphasize keeping the ball in play.

At this point, the instructor may repeat mini-drills in any problem areas to strengthen the players' skills. She emphasizes the importance of holding service as this is often not realized by non-racquet players. She reviews all rules and answers any questions on strategy or court positions that the players may have and stresses *consistency* and *concentration,* for they are the keys to improving the beginner's game.

Intermediate Play

As mentioned previously, we encourage players to sign up in foursomes at the intermediate level. The instructor may use whichever of the aforementioned drills she thinks suitable. Each player has her own technique and the instructor should be flexible in guiding her toward improvement of her specific shots and skills. During their playing times, strategy, combination of plays, change of pace, and techniques should all be discussed. Keeping the opponent off balance by mixing up the shots and doing the unexpected while still playing percentage shots are a must for these more advanced players. Also emphasize the importance of hitting *purposeful* shots. These can only be done by practice and more practice of the basic skills.

Tips for Success

1. Instructors should practice each drill before presenting it to a clinic.
2. Players should rotate between the deuce and ad courts at play times. At the end of four sessions, the instructor should have a feel for which side of the court a girl plays best and advise her to practice and improve on that side.
3. Instructors should suggest players compete in club tournaments and participate in league matches.
4. Instructors should not necessarily change a player's style with a particular shot if she is consistent and feels comfortable hitting it.
5. Instructors should encourage players to have their husbands or male friends join them on the courts.

....

Carrington Clark, Jr., a Cleveland, Ohio, stockbroker, was right in the middle of all the excitement when paddle was introduced in Cleveland. As a fine competitive player, fund raiser, salesman, organizer, promoter, tournament director, equipment distributor, raconteur, huckster, and hustler, Clark helped paddle become immensely popular in a very short period of time. He and his partner David Dickenson were the first midwestern duo ever to be ranked nationally in the Top Ten; they were ranked sixth in 1970 and eighth in 1971, and they were the top-ranked western team in 1972–1973. During the winter of 1972, they stunned the best teams by beating them en route to an impressive win in the important Short Hills (New Jersey) Invitational. Clark is an outstanding example of a nonnatural athlete becoming a top-flight tournament platform tennis player primarily through dedication, practice, persistence, and hard work.

20. | CARRINGTON CLARK, JR.

The Cleveland Story

IF ONE COULD ONLY MASTER half the skills described in this book, he would be a one-man, super-super-star — possibly destined and equipped never to lose another point. One constant theme seems to underline all the chapters, however, and that is practice, practice, work, and practice more in order to improve the basic skills of platform tennis.

At this particular stage in the growth and development of paddle, however, practice is not always possible. How does a transplanted New Yorker, for instance, practice these skills when suddenly he finds himself living in a city lacking a single platform tennis court? Only a few of his new-found friends have even heard of the game! As recently as 1967 rotted boards and saggy, rusted chicken wire were all that remained of the original court located on the grounds of the posh Chagrin Valley Hunt Club in Gates Mills, Ohio. Such a dismal-looking structure certainly betrayed the future glories of our favorite game in Cleveland. In the late forties paddle came to our city but died an early death. Tennis, polo, swimming, and, of course, the hunt were much too popular pastimes to compete with the little-known sport of platform tennis. Even the arrival of a former National champion, Witherbee Black from Rye, New York, was not enough to move the sport to the forefront.

Phase one of getting platform tennis started in a new area is quite obvious — courts have to be erected. Early during the summer of 1968 three courts were built in Cleveland. The first was a private court built by the late Mr. and Mrs. George E. Enos. Many Clevelanders hit their first platform tennis ball on this court. Then the Hunt Club's courts were constructed. They were built parallel to each other and about fifteen feet apart. On half the space between the courts a rustic warming hut was erected. It was a one-room, noninsulated building with large glass picture windows on each side for viewing the action of the courts. After a few nippy winters an excellent heater was installed. Tables and stools were put in the hut and the motif was warm and informal. The balance of the area between the courts was used by the more hearty spectators. Two very important precedents for future installations were set with this particular layout. At least *two* courts should be built at a club to aid and abet the establishing of a successful paddle program, and the building of a *warming hut* insures a place to thaw out, to greet, warm, party, watch, argue, or whatever. The social aspects of the game are every bit as important as the competitive play itself, and a warming hut in cold weather enhances the feeling of fraternalism and conviviality.

Platform tennis started with a flourish in the early fall of 1968. One enthusiast was successful in arranging a clinic and exhibition soon after the completion of the courts. Four top nationally ranked players from the east were flown out from New York to show the locals the finer points and appeals of the game. Roger Lankenau, Don Miller, Oliver Kimberly, and Dick Squires spent the weekend with us at the Hunt Club. A two-out-of-three-set exhibition was followed by an instructional clinic for all club enthusiasts. Men and women, boys and girls all took their turns hitting balls with the "pros."

Other Cleveland clubs followed this format when launching their platform tennis programs. Naturally the entire Hunt Club membership was invited to the inaugural exhibition, but *all* of Cleveland's clubs located on the east side were encouraged to attend. A bar was set up in the warming hut, and the club on opening day started to realize platform tennis revenues — regardless of how insignificant they may have seemed in proportion to the dollars expended on the facilities. A dinner was held at the club that evening for its members and guests that stimulated greater interest and enthusiasm and also generated additional income.

Another precedent was established when the Hunt Club paid the expenses for the out-of-town "stars." Any club that installs platform tennis courts for the first time should try to show its members platform tennis as it can and should be played by the best players around. The few dollars invested in sending for help was the best investment ever made for Cleveland paddle. We made friends with our teachers who, in turn, have repaid us a hundred times over in continuing friendships and active participation in all Cleveland tournaments since that opening day. The vital role of the Roger Lankenaus, the Dick Squires, the "Kim" Kimberlys, and the Donnie Millers to the Cleveland paddle scene can never be overstated or overestimated. This kick-off exhibition clinic was the catalyst that eventually brought on the explosion. We were properly introduced to paddle's unique strokes and strategies from the very start. We learned quickly, and, therefore, started having fun almost immediately.

The game had arrived, and now someone had to nurture, promote, and organize the sport. This was phase two. An athlete, who was also a professional public relations man, volunteered. He initiated a promotional campaign to bring paddle to The Country Club. The board of directors of his club came to "observe" and to play on the Hunt Club's courts. Our master promoter kept pressing and "selling," and finally the board agreed. The Country Club should have platform tennis! Two courts were built with a magnificent warming hut. One year later Cleveland had its first *four*-court facility. The game was instantly popular with The Country Club's members. The women cajoled Witherbee Black into providing them with morning instruction and all kinds of club tournaments were organized.

Two important things were accomplished the first year platform tennis was introduced at the club. Anyone remotely interested was instantly appointed to a committee and had to become "involved." In addition, a close financial check was kept to document the dollars brought into the club by paddle participators. Events were organized to the nth degree by hardworking committees. Men's, Women's, Mixed, Scrambles, Junior's, Member-Guest Invitationals, Handicaps were some of the tournaments scheduled. Especially popular were the

Wednesday-night Husband-Wife Mixed Doubles followed by a modest buffet dinner and much camaraderie. The board, armed with the necessary number of dinners bought and drinks purchased, was delighted to allocate funds for the two additional courts the following year. Interestingly enough, court usage at The Country Club increased dramatically (more than doubled!) when there were four courts as opposed to two.

Many ideas evolved from the early years of paddle at The Country Club that should be implemented by clubs in other areas just becoming interested in the sport. Nothing is a greater help than a formal program to promote the game. A large, working(!) committee and endless phone calls are important to the ultimate success of paddle. Accurate financial records showing the incremental revenues accruing to the club and directly related to platform tennis activity do much to generate enthusiasm and cooperation from the more conservative, cost-conscious board members. Local statistics have shown that a paddler will spend money on drinks, court time, guests, food, equipment, and instruction in much the same way a golfer does. They are similar types. The ancillary sociable aspects of the sport are almost as much fun as the sport itself.

The following year it was obvious that platform tennis in the Cleveland area was really beginning to erupt. Country clubs such as Kirtland, Mayfield, and Oakwood had their initial courts installed. After that it was merely a question of time and money that steered the course of paddle expansion in northeastern Ohio. A real problem, however, cropped up at this time. To the uninitiated the construction of a platform tennis court does not seem to be a very difficult project to tackle. To the casual eye it appears to be nothing more than a giant cage built out of wood and surrounded with chicken wire. But, believe me, looks can really be deceiving! Inexperienced contractors, off-season greenskeepers, and well-meaning club members should be avoided like the bubonic plague when it comes time to select a court builder. If nothing else is absorbed from this article, I beg you not to fall prey to the "let's-build-it-ourselves-and-save-a-few-bucks syndrome." A screen that cannot be tightened, glasslike surfaces that cannot be played on in a light drizzle, settling of the court's foundations, planks that warp and rot in a single season, etc., will inevitably mean an instant death to a club's new platform tennis program. Go to the professional and reputable court builders! The American Platform Tennis Association has a list of six or seven approved builders that they will, upon request, furnish to anyone.

Phase three occurred about three years after the Hunt Club's courts were installed. Paddle was off the ground, and nearly all eastside clubs either had built or were planning to build courts. Now came the $64.00 question: How are players developed and how is it possible to elevate the caliber of play locally — especially when there really aren't any teaching professionals around at this stage of the game's development? One of the first essential steps toward answering that question is to attract the best athletes in the area to the sport. If it is believed a particular area is too sports-saturated for the introduction of still another game, I offer the following facts about Cleveland: Kirtland has indoor tennis for its members during the winter months, Oakwood has squash, the Hunt Club offers indoor riding, the Cleveland Racquet Club has eight indoor tennis courts, four singles squash courts, and a doubles court, the Skating Club also has indoor tennis, Mayfield has an active curling program, and there are literally hundreds of outdoor tennis courts. Nonetheless, at all these clubs the paddle courts are "loaded" from eight in the morning until far into the frosty evenings!

One of Cleveland's very best tennis players, and more importantly a man destined to become this author's future paddle partner, became smitten with the sport. David Dickenson asked me to teach him everything necessary to be the best player in Cleveland and within a very brief period of time he was! When other fine tennis players heard that Dave had taken up paddle they, too, decided the game must have something.

The APTA decided to allow racquet professionals to play in tournaments and this encouraged several local teaching tennis pros to try it. John Brownlow, then the Skating Club tennis professional, took up platform tennis and quickly became a formidable player — first with Bob Reed and later with Scotty Rogers, the latter fresh out of Princeton. David and I worked hard enough at it to be ranked as high as sixth nationally and to also become the first noneastern team to win an APTA-sanctioned tournament. Brownlow and Rogers have not lost to another midwestern team to date and could be ranked in the top ten nationally in 1973-1974.

The women also began to see the appeals of paddle, and many top

Cleveland Invitational Directors (l. to r.) David S. Dickenson II, H. Richard Taylor, Willis M. McFarlane, Carrington Clark, Jr., Robert M. Bartholomew. (Missing from photo: John J. Bernet and John F. Turben.)

tennis players adopted the sport for the first time. Ann Kline and Ruth Sadler, both excellent tennis competitors, became the second non-eastern duo to win a major tournament, and their tennis rivals Barbara Allen and Sally Neville were an even match for them. The point here is that there developed a core of very fine male and female athletes who truly wanted to excel in paddle once they were exposed to it. Because of their fiery competitiveness they worked hard to improve their games. I predict there will be a National champion from Cleveland one of these days — perhaps he will be my grandson, but I don't believe it will take that long!

Besides attracting some of the better tennis players and athletes in the area, another important part of phase three is the organizing of competitive play. An interclub platform tennis league was founded and modeled after the highly successful Northern New Jersey format. The men's league is played one night a week, while the women compete in the mornings. Presently Cleveland has "A" and "B" leagues in order to better distribute the individual abilities of the players. In this way the newer players and clubs just getting started have the opportunity to spar with many different opponents and thereby upgrade their skills by competing against better players. As in any sport this is the key to improvement. Each club match consists of five doubles teams.

Perhaps the most important event contributing to the meteoric growth of paddle in Cleveland was the decision to hold a major tournament and invite some of the top players from New York, New Jersey, Connecticut, etc. The printed program for the first tournament in 1970 stated the goals of the Cleveland Invitational: (1) to bring the world's finest paddlers to Cleveland, (2) to improve the quality of paddle in Cleveland and throughout the entire midwest, and (3) to have an enjoyable weekend among ourselves and with our new friends. What was not written in the program was the fact that all Clevelanders would be getting together for the common purpose of promoting the game in our city. The tournament weekend was extremely successful. New lifelong friendships were formed and our platform tennis world continued to expand.

In the spring of 1973 we really hit the big time when Cleveland played host to the Men's National Doubles Championship — the first

The first time in thirty-nine years the APTA National Men's Doubles was not held at the Fox Meadow Club in Scarsdale, New York. The scene is a 1973 semifinal-round match between defending champions John Mangan and Bob Kingsbury (at net) against Doug Russell (1.) and blitzing Dick Squires at Cleveland's Racquet Club. The umbrellas indicate perfect paddle weather.

time in thirty-nine years that this prestigious event was not held at the game's founding club, Fox Meadow, in Scarsdale, New York. Four hundred and fifteen paddle competitors arrived from fifteen states for four days of wine and roses plus some highly competitive and great platform tennis. Food, drink, entertainment, transportation, and housing were a few of the miscellaneous details to be taken care of by our hardworking committees. During the endless planning sessions a company president said he would take charge of the finances to insure the success of the Nationals. Because of his business sense and acumen he was the perfect person to handle this phase of the tournament. The women also played enormously vital roles in making the tournament "the most auspicious and enjoyable Nationals ever." Cleveland's first Junior event in 1973 drew fifty-eight "eighteen and under" entrants from seven states — the largest draw to date in Junior platform tennis history!

A mere six years after the first platform tennis courts were installed and programs implemented, Cleveland now has over sixty courts and twelve warming huts! These represent a total investment of over $1,500,000. It is today almost impossible to find a country club without at least two courts. I hope as the game continues to explode that courts will be constructed at some of our local colleges, schools, and hotels. And when Cleveland's director of recreation orders some courts for the public parks and recreational areas, we will all know the sport has really "arrived." We will also have the immense satisfaction of knowing we helped to "plant the seeds."

The phases followed for developing paddle in Cleveland represent no magic formula. They would undoubtedly work successfully in San Francisco, Dallas, Atlanta, or, for that matter, in any city in America. When you really analyze the "overnight" success of platform tennis in Cleveland the real story is nothing more than a lot of people who grew to love the sport and were willing to work together to make it all happen. Usually things just don't happen — people make them happen.

R. Donald Barr, Executive Director of the Princeton, New Jersey, Recreation Department, is interested in paddle as well as in fishing, hunting, softball, basketball, golf, and tennis. He became enamored with platform tennis at thirty-seven, rather late in life. Under his leadership and organization, "public paddle" has literally "gone wild" in Princeton. In 1970–1971, he and his fellow recreator, Jack Roberts, set an example for the town by annexing Princeton's Men's League Doubles title. His paramount problem today is where to install much-needed additional courts.

21. | R. DONALD BARR

How To Implement a Community Platform Tennis Program

THE CONCEPT of community platform tennis is a relatively new one, but with the overwhelming response in several municipalities pioneering the idea, the future looks bright for "public paddle programs."

Since its inception back in 1928 platform tennis has been a sport associated with the "country club" set. The Recreation Department in Princeton, New Jersey, set out to change this image by constructing two municipal courts with taxpayers' money.

It is my hope that this chapter will provide food for thought and will convince taxpayers (and that covers most of us) and professional recreation directors throughout the country that platform tennis programs can be organized on a community level.

The sport is an excellent form of recreation that can be enjoyed by male and female, young and old, and rich, poor, or anyone in between. We have found that our public courts are in use twelve months a year and that during the hot summer they get quite a bit of play in the evening hours.

The events as they occurred in Princeton played a significant role in the formation of what we consider to be a successful platform tennis program. The techniques might very well differ slightly in other communities, but the overall approach should be quite similar. Community leaders attempting to organize paddle programs in their communities will have something additional going for them. They will be able to profit from other muncipalities that have already organized successful (either profitable or self-sustaining) community programs.

The idea that platform tennis courts would be a fine addition to our centrally located Community Park was first suggested to the Recreation Board in 1967 at a time when the sport was growing in popularity at country clubs. At the time the park facilities included a pool complex, a battery of fifteen tennis courts, and a number of multi-purpose ball fields. Any project of this magnitude requires extensive research and support before it can be sold to the governing body, which ultimately make the final decision on whether or not to appropriate funds. It is important that you "do your homework" and have the answers to the questions that will come up when you make your presentation to the governing body or in our case the governing bodies.

Princeton is actually two municipalities that have joined together for many of their services, recreation being one of them. The Recreation Board is made up of four representatives from the Borough and four representatives from the Township of Princeton approved by their respective governing body. This joint arrangement makes the process a little more complicated and requires approval from both municipalities before funds are appropriated.

It was in the research stage that I became painfully aware of the fact that very little had been written about implementing a community platform tennis program. In fact back in 1967 I couldn't locate a single municipality with public courts. This made our task a little more difficult and narrowed our research to area country clubs with platform tennis facilities. It was refreshing to find a number of area country club members who were ready, willing, and able to assist us with our community program, from the planning stage through the organization of leagues and assistance with setting up Townwide Tournaments. Such *planned competition* is an integral part of the ultimate success of a community platform tennis program.

A number of residents had been exposed to paddle as either members or guests at these clubs, so we already had one essential factor — the expression of enthusiastic interest. And we were able to gather information regarding construction costs and operating expenses from the local clubs. Now there was only one unknown factor: would this sport be popular on a communitywide basis? If we were to make the sizable investment to construct the courts, would we be able to establish a viable program or would we have two rather expensive white elephants on our hands? After all, the vast majority of our town citizens had never been exposed to the game. After thoroughly analyzing all the information we were able to gather, the Recreation Board unanimously agreed in 1969 to request the funds from the governing bodies to construct two courts.

We were all concerned about that one unknown factor: how will the community react to this new experience? Consequently, much thought went into what we could do to make the program successful. A definition of success would have to take into consideration participation and the entire financial picture.

The Recreation Board had established financial policies in regard to the specialized facilities, such as the pool complex and the tennis courts, and it used similar guidelines for the new platform tennis courts. The policy stated that having these facilities in Princeton made the community a better place in which to live and therefore the construction cost of these specialized facilities should be paid for through taxes. There are individuals living in Princeton who for one reason or another may not choose to use these facilities and they should not be further burdened by paying the annual operating expenses on these specialized facilities. These operating expenses should be met through user fees, not taxes. Although the fees were minimal they have accomplished their purpose each year since the policy was established.

The policy for platform tennis differs slightly from the other facilities in that the fee is for the privilege of making advanced reservations and not for use of the courts. Free time (other than prime-time hours) is indicated on the sign-up sheets, and play during this period is on a first-come-first-serve basis in one-and-one-half-hour blocks and is open to any Princeton resident. The original fee was $5.00 for the year, which entitled the individual to make advanced reservations. We knew from the experience of the area country clubs approximately what the operating expenses would be each year, and we set the fee based on projected participation. The figure we used back in 1969 was $1000 for operating expenses on the two courts; this included resurfacing the courts, new nets, and emergency repairs. We installed coin-operated lights, and the revenue from the lights paid for electricity and replacement of lamps.

We were looking for two hundred season-ticket-holders during the first season, and we realized that we had our work cut out for us to accomplish this goal. On the other hand, we had an obligation to the potential participants to keep the cost as low as possible while encouraging individuals to try their skill at this relatively new sport.

To officially open the courts Dick Squires, Chuck Baird, Richard Heath, and John S. McGeeney staged a demonstration of how to play platform tennis. The event was publicized in our local papers well in advance, which, along with excellent weather, accounted for a large turnout to witness the exhibition. The players explained what the game was all about and then proceeded to demonstrate the various strokes, strategies, and maneuvers associated with the sport. Watching the reaction of the spectators and listening to their questions after the exhibition I was confident we were off to a good start, but I also realized we still had a long way to go.

The Recreation Department purchased paddles and balls and made them available to individuals who wanted to try the game. We publicized the free use of equipment and emphasized that the game appeals to all ages, both sexes, and is an excellent form of family recreation. We used the public library to show films on platform tennis, and on each occasion we had a question and answer period at the conclusion of the film. We held clinics for everyone, and from these clinics we acquired a list of paddle enthusiasts.

Every community has its leaders and I would say Princeton is blessed with an abundance of leadership talent. We involved these individuals in setting up leagues for men, women, and couples. The first year we ran a rotation system in both the men's and women's leagues. The purpose was to make it possible for each player to have a different partner and two different opponents to play against each week. This is contrary to Dick Squires' philosophy on forming lasting partnerships, but our objective was to acquire paddle enthusiasts and the actual competition was secondary. This system accomplished its purpose, and because most of the participants were playing platform tennis for the first time the matchups were not that bad. We had some one-sided matches, particularly in the men's league, and these led to changes the following season.

The women's leagues still use the rotation system, and for some reason it seems to work out fine. They have eight women on a team and each individual plays with a different partner and two different opponents each week. The best way to describe this might be to say that the eight players constitute a league which continually rotates partners and opponents and the winners each week accumulate one point per set. At the conclusion of the season the two individuals with the greatest number of points on each of the ten teams participate in a tournament. The men's league seems to be more competitive and less social than the women's league, and a system of drafting seems to work best for them. We have at present seven teams of eight men per team and twenty-eight substitutes. On each of the seven teams we have first, second, third, and fourth doubles, each team competing in its own bracket against the matching doubles on the other six teams. One point is scored for each set won and the team (eight players) with the most points at the end of the season is the league champion. Competition through the drafting system is equalized and more appealing to the men. The couples league started with sixteen couples and has expanded to forty-eight, and there is a long waiting list.

As we did, you might arrange a program on platform tennis with a local TV station. The local high school included platform tennis as an elective in its physical education program, and we noticed students from Princeton University beginning to appear on the courts frequently.

By 1972 the two courts had reached their saturation point during prime-time hours and frustrated players were finding it increasingly difficult to reserve a court for a convenient time. Individuals and couples wanting to join the various leagues had to be put on waiting lists. The explosion of league play and free play, whether it was from our overzealous promotional campaign or just the natural appeal of paddle, left us with two alternatives — curtail programs or request funds for additional courts. The board once again contacted the governing bodies. The filled sign-up sheets documenting court use and the revenue proved to be extremely helpful in convincing the council and the committee of the need for two additional courts.

In an effort to slow down the increasing tax burden on the residents the governing bodies agreed to finance the project but asked the Recreation Board to revise its policy on the fee structure so that both capital and operating expenses would be met through user fees. The board agreed and once again we were off and running.

The two additional courts were installed, and we asked Dick Squires if he would set up the opening day ceremony. This time, however, we had two men and two women playing a match. Dick brought B. J. DeBree, Gloria Dillenbeck, and Doug Russell with him, and on a clear but extremely cold Sunday afternoon in December our two new courts were officially opened. A number of spectators sat through an exciting match even though the temperature was in the 'teens, and I would say the reason was their love for good platform tennis.

The two additional courts gave us the flexibility to run an expanded program and relieved at least temporarily the overly crowded conditions we were experiencing with just two courts. We have since added teams to all our leagues and have started a competitive program for women with matches set up on a home and away basis with area country clubs.

The courts are used extensively, and because they were constructed in an isolated area of the park the lights can be turned on at any hour. We have a number of commuters who play at 5:00 A.M., shower, and catch the train to either New York or Philadelphia.

An unusual event that has become extremely popular in Princeton is New Year's Eve paddle parties.

The highlight of the platform tennis season is the Townwide Tournament set up in March, which involves most of the players in the Princeton area. There are two tournaments, one for men and one for women, and the competition is excellent. A large number of spectators turns out to watch this event, which each year grows in size and stature.

The fee structure at present is $15.00 for an individual, $25.00 for a husband and wife, or $40.00 for an entire family. This fee, as I mentioned earlier, is for advanced registration privileges for a full year.

We have kept our moral obligation to the governing bodies in terms of revenue. In fact, our income for 1973 was $4850, which pays one fifteenth of the construction cost of all four courts as well as the operating expenses. What this means is with our present fee structure we can provide facilities to any Princeton resident and pay the cost off over a fifteen-year period with income derived from those individuals who are willing to pay for the privilege of making advance reservations.

The platform tennis courts provide a unique exposure to a fantastic sport on a community level. There is no way of knowing the exact number of participants on our courts because of our free-play policy, but we know at present 280 individuals participate in league play and their number increases each year.

A spot check of the courts might turn up a family on one court, four elderly individuals on another, two couples on a third, and four children on the fourth. A glance at the expressions on their faces indicate they are thoroughly enjoying themselves and, as far as I'm concerned, that's what recreation is all about.

These are the rules we've adopted. They can be used as guidelines for your new public platform tennis program:

1. Use of the courts is restricted to Princeton Borough and Township residents, season permit holders, employees, and members of official boards and commissions.
2. Yearly season tickets are available at the following rates:

Residents		Nonresidents (By Letter Only)	
Family (12 yrs. and over)	$40.00	Family	$80.00
Husband and Wife	25.00	Husband & Wife	50.00
Individual	15.00	Individual	30.00

3. Reservations will be accepted for the specified ticket holders for 1½ hour blocks as indicated on the sign-up sheets. The period between 12:30 P.M. and 5:00 P.M. is free to any Princeton resident regardless of whether they have a season ticket (*not weekends or holidays*). Free play is on a first come, first serve 1½-hour basis beginning at 12:30 P.M. The free-resident-time block will be open on *Courts 1 and 2 only*.
4. The names and season ticket numbers of each player must be listed for each reserved hour and a half. Reservations for less then four players is not permitted.
5. Those wishing to bring guests must sign "guests" for each guest player. The recreation department asks that members refrain from bringing guests on a regular basis.
6. Sign-up sheets will be posted on the bulletin board at the platform tennis courts one day in advance at 9:00 A.M. in the morning.
7. No person may play more than one period each day (more play is permitted if a player arrives at the courts and finds that a court has not been reserved).

8. Sneakers must be worn.
9. All other rules applicable to Community Park apply.
10. Lost season tickets will be replaced at the recreation office for a fee of $1.00.
11. There shall be no refunds of money paid for season tickets.
12. All injuries must be reported immediately to the recreation director.
13. The Princeton Recreation Department reserves the right to restrict prime time due to the formation of platform tennis leagues. All restricted times will be posted on the bulletin board prior to league play.
14. The platform tennis season for purposes of season tickets shall be from October 1 through September 30.

THE SEASON TICKET AND PLAYING PRIVILEGES OF PERSONS NOT OBSERVING THE FOREGOING RULES AND REGULATIONS ARE SUBJECT TO REVOCATION.

Net man controlling the opponents.

Paul G. Sullivan resides in Scarsdale, New York, the birthplace of platform tennis, and is a member of the founding club, Fox Meadow. He was President of the American Platform Tennis Association in 1965–1966, and in 1969, he and Bob Muth went to the semifinals of the National Men's Doubles. He is proud of originating and instituting the annual APTA Honor Awards — a tribute to players and workers who have made lasting contributions to the sport. In 1972 he was a referee at London's Wimbledon tennis championships. No one is more ably qualified than Paul to write about conducting successful tournaments.

22. | PAUL G. SULLIVAN

How To Organize and
Hold a Successful Tournament

THE GROWTH of platform tennis has greatly increased the size and types of tournaments played. We now have National championships in men's doubles, women's doubles, mixed doubles, boys' doubles, girls' doubles, junior veterans (forty-five and over), men's and women's seniors (fifty years and over), and even men's super seniors (sixty and over). These championships are run under the auspices of the American Platform Tennis Association — the governing body of the game.

In addition to these Nationals, many clubs run husband-wife, parent-child, and "scrambles" events for the sheer enjoyment of the game. One of the oldest of tournaments is the ever-popular scrambles or "jambles." Traditionally, men and women are paired by the Draw Committee according to playing ability. Contestants are ranked A to C and matched together to provide a balanced team. An A man player would be paired with a beginning C woman player and vice versa. Care is taken to be sure players are not from the same club or town. This adds to the sociability of the tournament and provides a method of meeting players from outside the normal playing circle. Matches are even and exciting. The opportunity for the poorer players to play with better players adds to the fun. A scrambles tournament is really a weekend social event usually augmented by a dinner dance on Saturday evening. The dance is enhanced by a well-schooled master of ceremonies who awards prizes for the "weakest backhand," "most footfaults," "biggest poacher," etc. Because of the balanced draw, the addition of out-of-towners, and the Saturday evening festivities, the scrambles is a favorite event wherever held.

A successful tournament has two constants — all are *doubles* tournaments and all require a dedicated tournament chairman. Today's best players discriminate between the badly organized and the well run. Thus, the balance of this chapter will provide the guidelines for a newly appointed chairman to follow.

You have just become tournament chairman for an invitational men's doubles event to be held at your club one weekend two months hence. Certainly you can't wait for things to happen. You immediately take step one — selecting a working committee and giving the members assignments.

Pick proven workers — club members who are noted for getting a job done. For a weekend tournament of sixty-four teams, you need the following assistants.

Invitation Chairman

He or she sends out the invitations six weeks prior to your selected date. The invitation should give date, place, time of play, cutoff date for replys, and any information of a social nature — notice of luncheons served, cocktails and dinner dances held in conjunction with the tournament, etc. The invitation should state the entry fee, return address, and telephone number to call for information in case of postponement due to weather. Once the notice is sent, the tournament is under way.

The tournament draw is a function of the teams invited. Go over the list with your invitation chairman to be certain the teams you wanted are invited. It's wise to follow up with a personal phone call to entrants. However, be firm about the cutoff date. Do not allow late entries. Players will respect decisiveness.

Bar Chairman

He or she controls all the hard liquor served. An open bar is disaster. A bar chairman can ruin his budget and damage the quality of play by serving too long. Bars should be open for no more than two or three hours during lunchtime only. Liquor should be bought on consignment and the unopened bottles returned. Otherwise, costs quickly get out of hand.

Parking Chairman

He or she is in charge of players and spectators who drive cars. The parking chairman should hire several teen-age club members to direct traffic and make the best use of available parking space. Added space near the club might need to be reserved so that residential streets are not clogged. The parking facilities at nearby schools and churches are often available on weekends.

Luncheon Chairman

The club will be providing luncheon for all entrants on Saturday and all remaining players on Sunday. Here the distaff side usually takes over. Select a devoted "paddle wife" to head your committee and leave her alone. Give her the number of players expected both days and let her do the rest. Women generally know best how to give buffet luncheons. You should inform her that serious players prefer soup, salad, and cold cuts to heavy meals. Some entrants won't eat at all. Coke, iced tea, and coffee are in big demand. Give your luncheon chairman an exact number of entrants well in advance to facilitate the ordering of supplies.

House Chairman

He or she is concerned with having your club facilities in top condition for your tournament. The house chairman will work in close rapport with the luncheon committee without invading its territory. He will be certain that coffee is available for the early rounders, that wood is in supply for the club fireplace, and that the men's locker room is clean and functioning. This includes plenty of soap and towels for the shower takers. The house chairman should have on hand a complete first-aid kit for scrapes and sprains. The ladies' locker room should supply the same plus hairpins, deodorant, and sanitary napkins. These items are easy to obtain and greatly appreciated. Tournament play can be strenuous, thus the completely equipped club has emergency oxygen and resuscitating equipment handy.

Grounds Chairman

This selectee is concerned with having your courts in top shape the day of the tournament. He or she should inspect all wires and have them tightened where needed. Touch-up painting should be performed well before the scheduled date of your tournament. He should also be charged with reserving extra courts at other clubs in the proximity should you need them for the first rounds.

Finally (for cold weather areas only), he should have an emergency snow-removal crew of younger club members ready and willing to get the snow off the courts should it snow heavily the day or the night before the tournament commences.

Prize Chairman

He or she will personally select and obtain the prizes. Give your prize chairman a budget and inform him that engraved silver is coveted but in this age of high prices pewter and etched glass are also appreciated. Four prizes are required (winners and runners-up). However, prizes of glassware have become popular for the finalists of the Consolation Tournament that is often run for first-round losers. The addition of the Consolation match assures every participant of at least two matches for his Saturday efforts.

Draw Chairman

The invitation listed a cutoff date for entries. This date should be eight to ten days prior to the tournament weekend. With all entries in, it is now time for the draw committee to do its important job. The draw chairman should appoint several knowledgeable players to help him. He should choose members who have a good sense of the invited players' abilities and have them research the entries to evaluate current play. Phone calls to other tournament chairmen and players can provide background information on all teams prior to making the draw. The "making of the draw" can take as long as four or five hours. Thus, the committee should meet the Sunday or Monday evening prior to the tournament date in order to complete its job.

All competitive tournaments should have a seeded draw. The number of seeded or ranking teams shall be determined by the committee. Teams should be seeded according to ability, using performance in other tournaments last year and this as a rule of thumb. As a guide to your draw committee on a point scale of 100, the following weightings should be considered:

45 - Team performance to date this year.
45 - Team performance in this tournament last year.
10 - Team performance in this tournament two years ago.

The judgment of the committee should prevail in setting the order of the seeds. When the draw is posted, a list of those teams that are seeded and the order in which they are ranked should be clearly posted also.

The proper placing of the "seeds" in a sixty-four-team draw is most important. The generally accepted rule is "one in eight," which means a sixty-four-team draw would have eight seeded teams. The "placing" of a second eight and possibly a third eight teams in the draw is often done. These teams are selected as potential contenders. A distinction between "seeding" and "placing" is that the seeds must be posted while the placed teams are not usually named.

Once the top eight seeds have been selected and ranked, the following rules must apply in placing their names in the draw: Numbers 1 and 2 shall be drawn by lot, the first drawn to be placed at the top of the upper half of the sixty-four-team draw sheet and the second at the bottom of the lower half. Numbers 3 and 4 are drawn by lot, the first drawn to be placed at the top of the second quarter, the second to be placed at the bottom of the third quarter. Numbers 5, 6, 7, and 8 are drawn by lot, the first drawn to be placed at the top of the second eight (in the top half of the draw), the second drawn at the bottom of the seventh eighth (in the bottom half of the draw), the third drawn to be placed at the top of the fourth eight (in the top half of the draw), and the fourth to be placed at the bottom of the fifth eight (in the bottom half of the draw).

Once the seeds are placed in the draw, you then take the second eight teams (9-16 in ranking) place them in a hat, draw the names, and put them in the draw as outlined above. The same procedure follows for the third eight teams.

The names of all remaining entries should then be written on separate cards, placed in a hat, drawn one by one, and placed in the remaining open positions in the draw in descending order from top to bottom.

Sometimes the chairman will not have a full draw to work with. He must then give "byes" into the second round to achieve an equal number of players on both sides of the draw. The rules on giving byes are specific. When the total number of entries is the power of 2, i.e., 8, 16, 32, 64, 128, there are no byes. When the entry list does not fit the above numbers exactly, merely substract the number of entries from the next higher power of 2. To illustrate, if there are 52 entries, subtract 52 from the next higher power of 2, which is 64. Thus, there are 12 byes. Place these byes evenly in the draw. Six in the top half, six in the bottom. Give the 8 seeds the byes, and the 4 leftover byes go to the first two teams drawn "out of the hat" in the top half of the draw and the last two teams drawn into the bottom half of the draw.

The committee can exercise discretion when drawing the unseeded teams out of the hat by bypassing a team when it means that two opposing teams would include players from the same family, club, or city. In this case, the second team drawn can be placed in the same relative position in the next quarter of the draw. A tournament draw that satisfies everyone is dependent upon the work of this committee. By following the above procedures the chairman can minimize criticism from overzealous players or the perpetual bellyachers.

The committee's final function on this long evening is to schedule matches and notify the players. It is wise to set first-round matches for no later than 9:00 A.M. Try to avoid scheduling an early match for a team that must travel a long distance. Remember that a sixty-four-team event requires six rounds to complete. Four rounds of play should be scheduled on Saturday with the semis and finals on Sunday. Have all avaliable courts in use for first-round matches and so notify these early birds by postcard. These postcards should be mailed *at least* five days prior to Tournament Saturday to assure delivery. All postcards should clearly show place and match time as well as warn of an automatic default for a fifteen minute lateness.

Tournament Day

Tournament Saturday has arrived and the chairman and aides must be at the club early. The hours between 9:00 A.M. and noon are vital and require the total commitment and energies of all concerned. Players must be checked in, given locker assignments, name tags, and luncheon tickets and be shepherded to their assigned court promptly. As chairman, you must take full responsibility to default late arrivals. Tardiness is not fair to the players and can raise havoc with the schedule. With sixty-four entrants, the first two rounds should be completed by twelve noon. This brings the tournament to the round of sixteen. The luncheon chairman and bar chairman serve promptly from twelve to 2:00 P.M. The round of sixteen should be scheduled for 2:00 P.M. Thus, the quarter finals (round of eight) can start by 3:15. Be conscious that the winter days are short and sufficient daylight can be a problem. However, most clubs have night lights available. It is the tournament chairman's decision when to use them and he must be objective and try to order lights on only prior to the start of a match or set. As chairman, you must exercise your authority to keep matches going, resolve disputes, and generally run the day. You cannot allow players to wander off club grounds. It is wise to have two copies of the draw — one outside near the courts and one inside the clubhouse. Aides should be assigned to record match results and keep these draws current. Set up your chairman's desk near the courts with a loudspeaker system to announce match assignments. Balls should be kept at room temperature. This can be accomplished by keeping the tournament balls in a heated container when outside or simply distributing match balls to players in your clubhouse.

As first-round matches are completed, ask the losing teams if they wish to enter the Consolation Tournament. Record all entries as they finish and place their names in the consolation draw in declining order from top to bottom. This added event provides enjoyment for the players with very little extra effort. Use the less worn tournament balls left over from the opening rounds and start the consolation matches only after the first two rounds of the main tournament are complete. Ask an assistant to take over this event and make match assignments as courts become free. You will find that many consolation matches can be completed during the noon to 2:00 P.M. lunch break.

At the end of play Saturday four teams will be left in the tournament — the semifinalists. You can instruct your consolation chairman to keep play going under lights to accomplish the same — four semifinalists. These matches should be set for Sunday morning — consolation semis at 10:00 A.M. and main event semis at 11:00 A.M. Finals should be scheduled for 1:00 and 2:00 P.M. respectively. With this done, it is now time to relax and enjoy the dinner dance being held by the club in conjunction with the tournament.

Sunday morning you and your committee should again be early birds. Allow time to get things in order for the day. Coffee should be available for players, wives, and spectators. The crowd will build as churchgoers come from morning services to see the play. Select an umpire for each semifinal and instruct him to gather his team of linesmen. These should be culled from experienced players who understand the rules and make their calls clearly and quickly. A well-umpired match runs smoothly, but inexperience can disrupt play. Control of the net position in platform tennis is of great importance. The chronic foot faulter who touches or steps into the court prior to striking the ball is taking very unfair advantage while assuming his net position. Instruct your linesmen to call foot faults as they see them. Top players will appreciate your decisiveness on this point. They wish to win but only within these rules.

The semifinals are over and it is time again for the luncheon chairman to perform. "Bull shots" (vodka and beef broth) are traditional for the Sunday brunch. Of course, the finalists will use this time to shower and prepare for the big match. Be sure to invite the individual umpiring the finals to Sunday lunch. This is a fine time for him to get to know the players and the clubs they represent. Until such time as the American Platform Tennis Association organizes an official umpires association, the individual chosen to officiate should be a qualified member of a regional Tennis Umpires Association.

By 2:00 P.M., the consolation finals are completed, prizes awarded, and luncheons with bull shots behind you. It is time for the finals. With linesmen in place, new balls available, and the trophies in full view of the crowd, you should present the umpire to the spectators. Be brief, for he must then get on with introducing the players and running the three-out-of-five-set match (for women's, juniors, seniors, and mixed doubles, two-out-of-three sets). At the finish you make the presentations to the winners and runners-up. This is also the time to compliment your committee members and all who have helped make this weekend event memorable.

Sunday evening is time for a quiet cocktail with your family. It is also a time for reflection. A team effort on the part of at least twelve persons was required. Your administrative abilities were tested and proven worthy. You have earned the respect of players, committee members, and club members alike — the job of tournament chairman has its rewards.

Platform Tennis Playing Rules

Except as otherwise noted, the rules of play and scoring of the United States Lawn Tennis Association shall govern.

1. *Balls off screens*

   If a ball in play or on the serve hits the deck in the proper court and then touches any part of the back or side screens including horizontal top or bottom members of the superstructure, it may be played, so long as it has not hit the deck a second time on the same side of the net.

2. *Only one serve*

   Only one serve is allowed. If the serve is a fault, the server loses that point.

3. *Balls bounced over back or side screens*

   Balls which are bounced over the screen after bouncing fairly in opponent's court, or which hit an obstruction overhanging the court such as a tree or supporting bar across the corner, are to be considered "let balls" and the point played over again.

4. *Use of balls in tournaments*

   One ball only shall be used continuously during each set unless otherwise specified by the tournament committee. Server may not

substitute another ball during an unfinished set without the permission of the tournament officials, nor may server hold two balls
when serving.

5. *Number of sets in championship play*

This is to be specified for each National Championship tournament by the American Platform Tennis Association. (However,
the usual practice is to play two out of three sets in all but the
quarter-finals, semi-finals and finals of the National Men's Doubles,
when it is three sets out of five.)

6. *Foot faults*

The server shall throughout his delivery (moment of impact of
paddle and ball) of his service:

A. Not change his position by walking or running. The server
shall not by the following movements of his feet be deemed
"to change his position by walking or running."

1. Slight movements of the feet which do not materially affect the
location originally taken by him.
2. An unrestricted movement of one foot so long as the other foot
maintains continuously its original contact with the deck. The
moving foot cannot touch the base line or touch inside the
court before impact of paddle and ball.
3. Leaving the deck with both feet unless before the moment of
impact of paddle and ball either foot makes contact with the
base line or inside the court.

B. Not touch, with either foot, any area other than that behind
the base line within the imaginary extension of the center service line and the outer sideline.

7. *Good return*

It is a good return:

A. If the ball touches the net, posts, cord or metal cable, strap or
band, provided that it passes over any of them and hits the
deck within the court; or

B. If the ball, served or returned, hits the deck within the proper
court and rebounds or is blown back over the net, and the

player whose turn it is to strike reaches over the net and plays the ball, provided that neither he nor any part of his clothes or paddle touch the net, posts, cord or metal cable, strap or band or the deck within his opponents' court, and that the stroke is otherwise good; or

C. If the ball is returned outside the post, either above or below the level of the top of the net, whether or not it touches the post, provided that it hits the deck within the proper courts; or

D. If a player's paddle passes over the net after he has returned the ball, provided the ball passes the net before being played by him and is properly returned.

8. *The APTA approved nine-point tiebreak*

The usage of the tiebreak is at the option of the tournament committee.

A. The nine-point tiebreak is played when games reach 6-all.

B. The player whose turn it is to serve the next regular game is the first server. This is always the same player who started serving the set.

C. The team that wins 5 points is the winner of the set. The set is scored 7–6.

D. Each player must serve from the same end of the court in the tiebreak that he or she has served from during the set. (Note that this alters the sequence of serving by the partners on the second serving team.)

For illustration, with the serving team designated as Players A and B, and their opponents as C and D, the service order is as follows:

> *Points 1 and 2* are served by player A. Player A is always the player who started serving the set.

TEAMS DO *NOT* CHANGE COURTS

> *Points 3 and 4* are served by player D (out of normal sequence, but the player who *normally served from that end*).

TEAMS CHANGE COURTS

Points 5 and 6 are served by player B.

Points 7 and 8 are served by player C.

Point 9   is served, if necessary, by player C, if the point score reaches 4-all. For this point only, the receiving team has the choice of receiving in either right court or left court.

E. To begin the next set, "stay for one" after the tiebreak. The team that *did not* serve first in the tiebreak serves first in the next set. Note that this rule continues to apply no matter how many sets in a match are decided by tiebreak.

APTA Honor Award Winners

On February 18, 1965, the Executive Committee of the APTA inaugurated the APTA Honor Award. The following individuals have made significant contributions to the game of platform tennis. Some of these people have contributed technically, some were founders and developers of the game. Some have been champion players and others have been doers. All of them have done most for platform tennis and have helped to make the game what it is today.

1965
Mrs. T. Edmund Beck
Fessenden S. Blanchard *
James K. Cogswell, Jr.*
Clifford Couch
Mrs. Percival S. Fuller *
Earle Gatchell *
Richard K. Hebard
Charles O'Hearn
Kenneth Ward

1966
James M. Carlisle
Donald K. Evans
Harold Holmes *
Mrs. William Koegel *
Mrs. S. Warren Lee
Mrs. Charles H. Walker
Frederick B. Walker *

1967
Walter H. Close
John A. Stephenson
Clifford S. Sutter

1968
Oscar F. Moore

1969
George R. Harrison
William E. Pardoe

1970
Mrs. Ronald Carroll
Alexander H. Carver, Jr.
Mrs. Mary Moore

1971
no presentation

1972
Philip Osborne

1973
Gordon S. Gray

1974
Richard J. Reilly, Jr.

1975
no presentation

1976
John Randolph Moses
Susan Beck Wasch

* Deceased

APTA Tournament Records

National Men's Doubles

Year	Winners	Runners-up	Score
1935	Clifford D. Couch, Jr. Sumner D. Kilmarx	James N. Hynson Charles M. O'Hearn	4-6, 6-4, 6-3 2-6, 9-7
1936	Harold D. Holmes Richard G. Newell	Fessenden S. Blanchard Earle Gatchell	3-6, 8-6, 4-6 9-7, 15-13
1937	James N. Hynson Charles M. O'Hearn	Clifford D. Couch, Jr. Sumner D. Kilmarx	6-1, 6-3, 6-0
1938	James N. Hynson Charles M. O'Hearn	A. Keith Eaton Donald M. White	6-8, 6-2, 6-3 3-6, 6-4
1939	Clifford D. Couch, Jr. Sumner D. Kilmarx	James N. Hynson Charles M. O'Hearn	6-3, 6-2, 5-7 6-3
1940	Witherbee Black, Jr. Paul de F. Hicks	C. E. Grafmueller James N. Landauer	6-3, 6-4, 1-6 7-5
1941	Joseph B. Maguire Clifford S. Sutter	Holbrook H. Hyde Leland Wiley	6-0, 6-8, 6-4 6-2
1942	Holbrook H. Hyde Leland Wiley	Witherbee Black, Jr. Paul de F. Hicks	6-3, 7-5, 7-9 2-6, 6-3
1943	Charles M. O'Hearn Donald M. White	Robert Lincoln John Moses	6-3, 3-6, 6-2 6-3
1944	Holbrook H. Hyde Leland Wiley	Witherbee Black, Jr. Paul de F. Hicks	6-4, 6-2, 6-4
1945	Joseph B. Maguire Clifford S. Sutter	Clifford D. Couch, Jr. Charles M. O'Hearn	6-1, 6-2, 6-1
1946	Joseph B. Maguire Clifford S. Sutter	Clifford D. Couch, Jr. Charles M. O'Hearn	5-7, 3-6, 6-1 6-2, 6-4
1947	John Grout John R. Moses	Holbrook H. Hyde Leland Wiley	2-6, 6-3, 6-3 6-0
1948	Clifford D. Couch, Jr. Charles M. O'Hearn	Rawle Deland John R. Moses	3-6, 8-6, 7-5 4-6, 12-10
1949	Richard K. Hebard Frederick B. Walker	Clifford D. Couch, Jr. Charles M. O'Hearn	9-11, 6-1, 6-3 6-1
1950	Clifford S. Sutter Sidney B. Wood	Gordon W. Sanford Addison R. Wilson	6-3, 6-1, 6-4
1951	Richard K. Hebard Frederick B. Walker	Daniel L. Dyer George R. Harrison	6-3, 6-4, 6-3
1952	Richard K. Hebard Frederick B. Walker	Daniel L. Dyer James P. Gordon	3-6, 7-5, 6-3 6-3
1953	Frank D. Guernsey W. Donald McNeill	Rawle Deland John R. Moses	2-6, 6-1, 6-4 3-6, 6-0

1954	Frank D. Guernsey	James M. Carlisle	3-6, 5-7, 14-12
	W. Donald McNeill	Richard K. Hebard	9-7, 6-2
1955	James M. Carlisle	Rawle Deland	8-6, 8-10, 6-1
	Richard K. Hebard	John R. Moses	8-6
1956	George R. Harrison	W. Donald McNeill	6-3, 2-6, 6-4
	William E. Pardoe	Herman A. Schaefer	6-4
1957	Frank D. Guernsey	James P. Gordon	7-5, 6-0, 4-6
	John R. Moses	Edward Yeaw, Jr.	6-3
1958	James M. Carlisle	George R. Harrison	4-6, 4-6, 7-5
	Richard K. Hebard	William E. Pardoe	7-5, 6-3
1959	William M. Cooper, Jr.	James M. Carlisle	3-6, 6-2, 6-2
	James P. Gordon	Richard K. Hebard	5-7, 8-6
1960	William E. Pardoe	W. Donald McNeill	7-5, 7-9, 6-4
	George R. Harrison	Frank D. Guernsey	6-3
1961	Richard K. Hebard	Edward L. Winpenny, Jr.	8-6, 6-2, 2-6
	A. H. Carver, Jr.	Edmund R. Swanberg	6-8, 6-3
1962	Richard K. Hebard	Edward L. Winpenny, Jr.	7-9, 6-0, 6-4
	A. H. Carver, Jr.	Edmund R. Swanberg	6-1
1963	Richard K. Hebard	Oliver A. Kimberly, Jr.	6-2, 7-5, 7-5
	A. H. Carver, Jr.	David Jennings	
1964	Oliver A. Kimberly, Jr.	Thomas Holmes	6-3, 6-1, 6-3
	David Jennings	Michael O'Hearn	
1965	Thomas Holmes	Edward L. Winpenny, Jr.	4-6, 6-3, 2-6
	Michael O'Hearn	Richard Squires	6-3, 6-2
1966	Edward L Winpenny, Jr.	Gordon Gray	6-4, 6-1, 6-2
	Richard Squires	Jesse F. Sammis III	
1967	Oliver A. Kimberly, Jr.	Edmund R. Swanberg	6-4, 2-6, 6-0
	David Jennings	Thomas C. Richardson	6-4
1968	Bradley Drowne	Gordon Gray	6-4, 6-2, 6-2
	William Scarlett	Jesse Sammis III	
1969	Gordon Gray	Bradley Drowne	6-1, 7-5, 3-6
	Jesse Sammis III	William Scarlett	8-6
1970	Gordon Gray	Robert Kingsbury	4-6, 6-4, 6-4
	Jesse Sammis III	John Mangan	2-6, 6-4
1971	Gordon Gray	Robert Kingsbury	3-6, 7-5, 6-4
	Jesse Sammis III	John Mangan	6-2
1972	John Mangan	Jesse Sammis III	6-4, 6-1, 6-1
	Robert Kingsbury	Gordon Gray	
1973	John Mangan	Keith Jennings	5-7, 6-3, 7-5
	Robert Kingsbury	Chauncy Steele	3-6, 6-4
1974	John Beck	Keith Jennings	7-5, 4-6, 6-2
	Herbert FitzGibbon II	Chauncy Steele	4-6, 6-2
1975	Keith Jennings	Robert Kingsbury	6-4, 6-3, 8-6
	Chauncy Steele	John Mangan	
1976	Steve Baird	Keith Jennings	6-4, 4-6, 6-3,
	Chip Baird	Chauncy Steele	7-5
1977	Herbert FitzGibbon, II	Douglas Russell	6-3, 7-5, 1-6,
	Hank Irvine	Gordon Gray	6-4

National Mixed Doubles

Year	Winners	Runners-up	Score
1935	Charles M. O'Hearn	Mr. and Mrs.	6-4, 4-6, 6-3
	Mrs. Percival S. Fuller	Clifford D. Couch, Jr.	

1936	Mr. and Mrs. Charles M. O'Hearn	Mr. and Mrs. Percival S. Fuller	6-3, 6-4
1937	Mr. and Mrs. Charles M. O'Hearn	C. E. Grafmueller Mrs. Edward Selden	6-3, 6-4
1938	Mr. and Mrs. Charles M. O'Hearn	C. E. Grafmueller Mrs. Edward Selden	6-2, 6-2
1939	Mr. and Mrs. T. Edmund Beck	Donald M. White Mrs. Oscar F. Moore	8-6, 2-6, 6-4
1940	Mr. and Mrs. Charles M. O'Hearn	Mr. and Mrs. T. Edmund Beck	6-3, 6-1
1941	Clifford S. Sutter Mrs. J. B. Maguire	Mr. and Mrs. T. Edmund Beck	6-3, 1-6, 6-2
1942	Paul de F. Hicks Mrs. Burr Price	Mr. and Mrs. Clifford S. Sutter	6-2, 0-6, 10-8

1943, 1944, 1945 This tournament was omitted, because of wartime travel difficulties due to gas shortage.

1946	Lamar M. Fearing Mrs. Oscar F. Moore	Addison R. Wilson Mrs. T. Edmund Beck	6-3, 4-6, 14-12
1947	Mr. and Mrs. Elwood T. Cooke (Sarah Palfrey)	A. Keith Eaton Mrs. Charles H. Walker	6-2, 6-0

1948 No record of a tournament for this year.

1949	Mr. and Mrs. Ronald Carroll	Mr. and Mrs. Stuart A. Lyman	6-4, 2-6, 6-3
1950	Mr. and Mrs. Ronald Carroll	Gordon W. Sanford Mrs. T. Edmund Beck	6-4, 4-6, 8-6
1951	Mr. and Mrs. Ronald Carroll	Richard K. Hebard Mrs. Oscar F. Moore	3-6, 6-3, 6-3
1952	Mr. and Mrs. Ronald Carroll	Frederick B. Walker Mrs. T. Edmund Beck	3-6, 6-4, 6-3
1953	Richard K. Hebard Mrs. T. Edmund Beck	Mr. and Mrs. Ronald Carroll	6-2, 6-4
1954	Richard K. Hebard Mrs. T. Edmund Beck	Mr. and Mrs. John Cookman	6-8, 6-2, 6-3
1955	John R. Moses Mrs. Frank Smith	Richard K. Hebard Mrs. T. Edmund Beck	6-3, 3-6, 6-4
1956	Richard K. Hebard Mrs. T. Edmund Beck	John R. Moses Mrs. Frank Smith	6-3, 6-3
1957	Richard K. Hebard Miss Ruth Chalmers	James M. Carlisle Miss Susan Beck	6-3, 6-2
1958	Edward L. Winpenny, Jr. Mrs. Edward A. Raymond	A. H. Carver, Jr. Mrs. Ronald Carroll	4-6, 6-1, 6-2
1959	George F. Lowman Mrs. Peyton C. Auxford	William E. Pardoe Mrs. David Harris	6-2, 6-3
1960	Clifford S. Sutter Suzanne Sutter	John Beck Mrs. William Wasch	3-6, 6-4, 6-3
1961	James P. Gordon Mrs. S. Warren Lee	Edward L. Winpenny, Jr. Mrs. Edward A. Raymond	8-6, 6-2
1962	James P. Gordon Mrs. S. Warren Lee	A. H. Carver, Jr. Mrs. William Koegel	8-6, 6-3
1963	Richard K. Hebard Mrs. S. Warren Lee	A. H. Carver, Jr. Mrs. William Koegel	6-4, 6-4

1964	A. H. Carver, Jr.	James P. Gordon	8-10, 11-9
	Mrs. William Koegel	Mrs. S. Warren Lee	6-1
1965	William Pardoe	John Beck	6-4, 6-2
	Mrs. S. Warren Lee	Mrs. William Wasch	
1966	Gordon Gray	William E. Pardoe	6-3, 6-4
	Mrs. William G. Symmers	Mrs. S. Warren Lee	
1967	Gordon Gray	Richard Squires	6-1, 6-4
	Mrs. William G. Symmers	Mrs. S. Warren Lee	
1968	Gordon Gray	A. H. Carver, Jr.	6-4, 6-3
	Mrs. William Symmers	Mrs. S. Warren Lee	
1969	Bradley Drowne	William Breed	6-4, 6-3
	Mrs. S. Warren Lee	Mrs. Charles Stanton	
1970	John Mangan	Bradley Drowne	6-2, 7-5
	Mrs. David Harris	Mrs. S. Warren Lee	
1971	Oliver A. Kimberly, Jr.	David McKissock	6-1, 6-3
	Mrs. Allan Hannas	Mrs. Ronald DeBree	
1972	John Beck	Michael North	8-6, 6-4
	Mrs. William Wasch	Mrs. Raymond O'Connell	
1973	Cecil North	John Beck	6-1, 14-12
	Isabel O'Connell	Mrs. William Wasch	
1974	Bradley Drowne	John Mangan	8-6, 7-5
	Mrs. Ronald DeBree	Mrs. Joseph Dillenbeck	
1975	Herbert FitzGibbon, II	John Mangan	**6-2, 6-1**
	Mrs. Ronald DeBree	Mrs. Joseph Dillenbeck	
1976	Herbert FitzGibbon, II	Hank Irvine	6-4, 6-4
	Mrs. Ronald DeBree	Nancy Mangan	
1977	Douglas Russell	Herbert FitzGibbon, II	1-6, 6-3, 7-5
	Hilary Hilton	Mrs. Ronald DeBree	

National Women's Doubles

Year	Winners	Runners-up	Score
1935	Mrs. Henry B. Eaton	Mrs. F. M. Hampton	6-1, 6-1
	Mrs. Percival S. Fuller	Mrs. G. S. Rockefeller	
1936	Mrs. Henry B. Eaton	Mrs. P. S. Bush	8-10, 6-1, 6-3
	Mrs. Percival S. Fuller	Mrs. William Wilson	
1937	Miss Sally Childress	Mrs. Edward Selden	8-6, 6-3
	Mrs. Oscar F. Moore	Miss Eugenie Thebaud	
1938	Mrs. T. Edmund Beck	Mrs. Percival S. Fuller	9-7, 6-3
	Mrs. C. H. Walker	Mrs. Charles M. O'Hearn	
1939	Mrs. T. Edmund Beck	Mrs. Percival S. Fuller	9-7, 6-3
	Mrs. C. H. Walker	Mrs. Charles M. O'Hearn	
1940	Mrs. T. Edmund Beck	Mrs. Oscar F. Moore	6-2, 6-3
	Mrs. C. H. Walker	Mrs. Burr Price	
1941	Mrs. T. Edmund Beck	Mrs. Oscar F. Moore	7-5, 6-2
	Mrs. C. H. Walker	Mrs. Burr Price	
1942	Mrs. T. Edmund Beck	Mrs. Oscar F. Moore	6-2, 4-6, 6-3
	Mrs. C. H. Walker	Mrs. Burr Price	

1943, 1944, 1945 Omitted because of wartime travel difficulties.

1946, 1947, 1948 Tournament not played

1949	Mrs. T. Edmund Beck	Mrs. Percival S. Fuller	6-3, 6-3
	Mrs. Oscar F. Moore	Mrs. Charles O'Hearn	
1950	Mrs. Ronald Carroll	Mrs. T. Edmund Beck	6-2, 6-2
	Mrs. August Ganzenmueller	Mrs. Oscar F. Moore	

1951	Mrs. T. Edmund Beck	Mrs. Ronald Carroll	6-3, 6-3
	Mrs. Oscar F. Moore	Miss Geraldine Mallory	
1952	Mrs. T. Edmund Beck	Mrs. Ronald Carroll	6-3, 6-3
	Mrs. Oscar F. Moore	Mrs. August Ganzenmueller	
1953	Mrs. T. Edmund Beck	Mrs. Ronald Carroll	6-1, 7-5
	Mrs. Oscar F. Moore	Mrs. August Ganzenmueller	
1954	Mrs. T. Edmund Beck	Mrs. William F. Koegel	6-1, 6-1
	Mrs. Oscar F. Moore	Mrs. John A. Schwable	
1955	Mrs. Ronald Carroll	Mrs. Peyton C. Auxford	6-4, 6-2
	Mrs. August Ganzenmueller	Mrs. T. Edmund Beck	
1956	Mrs. Peyton C. Auxford	Mrs. T. Edmund Beck	6-3, 6-4
	Mrs. William Koegel	Mrs. Frederick B. Walker	
1957	Mrs. Edward A. Raymond	Mrs. Ronald Carroll	6-2, 6-4
	Mrs. John A. Schwable	Mrs. August Ganzenmueller	
1958	Mrs. Ronald Carroll	Mrs. E. L. Bermingham	6-1, 10-8
	Mrs. August Ganzenmueller	Mrs. Edward A. Raymond	
1959	Mrs. T. Edmund Beck	Mrs. William Koegel	6-2, 3-6, 6-2
	Mrs. W. (Susan Beck) Wasch	Mrs. Frederick B. Walker	
1960	Mrs. T. Edmund Beck	Mrs. Ronald Carroll	6-1, 6-3
	Mrs. William Wasch	Mrs. August Ganzenmueller	
1961	Mrs. S. Warren Lee	Mrs. Peyton C. Auxford	4-6, 6-4, 6-4
	Mrs. Charles Sager	Mrs. F. A. Waterman	
1962	Mrs. Rawle Deland	Mrs. David Harris	4-6, 6-1, 7-5
	Mrs. William Wasch	Mrs. Edgar Nelson	
1963	Mrs. S. Warren Lee	Mrs. William Koegel	6-1, 6-2
	Mrs. Bradley Briggs	Mrs. Peyton C. Auxford	
1964	Mrs. S. Warren Lee	Mrs. Rawle Deland	4-6, 6-2, 6-1
	Mrs. Bradley Briggs	Mrs. William Wasch	
1965	Mrs. Rawle Deland	Mrs. S. Warren Lee	0-6, 9-7, 6-4
	Mrs. William Wasch	Mrs. Edmund Cox	
1966	Mrs. Edgar Nelson	Mrs. Garth Kauffman	6-4, 4-6, 6-3
	Mrs. S. Warren Lee	Mrs. William Symmers	
1967	Mrs. S. Warren Lee	Mrs. William Wasch	6-3, 6-2
	Mrs. Charles Stanton	Mrs. Rawle Deland	
1968	Mrs. S. Warren Lee	Mrs. W. Bradford Briggs	6-1, 10-8
	Mrs. Charles Stanton	Mrs. Rawle Deland	
1969	Mrs. Charles Stanton	Mrs. Joseph Dillenbeck	6-4, 6-3
	Mrs. S. Warren Lee	Mrs. Garth Kauffman	
1970	Mrs. Charles Stanton	Mrs. Allan Hannas	4-6, 6-0, 6-4
	Mrs. S. Warren Lee	Mrs. Hatsy Hart	
1971	Mrs. Joseph Dillenbeck	Mrs. S. Warren Lee	7-5, 4-6, 6-4
	Mrs. Ronald DeBree	Mrs. Charles Stanton	
1972	Mrs. Joseph Dillenbeck	Mrs. S. Warren Lee	6-3, 4-6, 6-4
	Mrs. Ronald DeBree	Mrs. Allan Hannas	
1973	Mrs. Joseph Dillenbeck	Mrs. Shirley Babington	2-6, 6-4, 6-3
	Mrs. Ronald DeBree	Mrs. Marti Cavanaugh	
1974	Mrs. Shirley Babington	Mrs. Joseph Dillenbeck	6-2, 6-0
	Mrs. Marti Cavanaugh	Mrs. Ronald DeBree	
1975	Hilary Hilton	Mrs. Shirley Babington	6-4, 6-3
	Annabel Lang	Mrs. Marti Cavanaugh	
1976	Wendy Chase	Mrs. Ronald DeBree	6-2, 7-6
	Linda Wolf	Fay Gambee	
1977	Louise Gengler	Mrs. Shirley Babington	6-2, 6-4
	Hilary Hilton	Mrs. Marti Cavanaugh	

National Senior Men's Doubles (age 50 or over)

Year	Winners	Runners-up	Score
1957	James M. Carlisle Berkeley D. Johnson	Charles W. Barnes, Jr. Gordon W. Sanford	6-1, 6-3
1958	James M. Carlisle Berkeley D. Johnson	Frank Pace, Jr. Clifford S. Sutter	6-2, 3-6, 7-5
1959	Frank Pace, Jr. Clifford S. Sutter	James M. Carlisle Berkeley D. Johnson	6-0, 6-3
1960	Walter H. Close Richard K. Hebard	Berkeley D. Johnson Harrison Cole	6-2, 6-4
1961	Walter H. Close Richard K. Hebard	William Pardoe Berkeley D. Johnson	0-6, 6-4, 6-3
1962	L. S. Bowen Sidney Sweet, Jr.	William Pardoe Berkeley D. Johnson	6-4, 1-6, 6-1
1963	A. H. Carver, Jr. George Harrison	Phil Steckler Irving Kram	5-7, 6-2, 6-3
1964	Germain Glidden William Park	Berkeley D. Johnson Charles Buchler	7-5, 8-6
1965	Richard K. Hebard Sidney Sweet, Jr.	Kenneth LaVine Harrison Cole	6-1, 6-1
1966	William E. Pardoe George Lowman	William Park Mansfield Sprague	6-2, 6-1
1967	William E. Pardoe George Lowman	Richard K. Hebard Donald Wheaton	6-2, 6-0
1968	George Lowman William Pardoe	Zan Carver George Harrison	4-6, 7-5, 6-1
1969	Ledyard S. Bowen Sidney Sweet, Jr.	Charles Dederick Peter Shonk	6-4, 6-4
1970	Richard K. Hebard Alexander H. Carver, Jr.	Ledyard S. Bowen Sidney Sweet, Jr.	6-3, 8-6
1971	Robert Baldwin George Schmid	Ledyard S. Bowen Sidney Sweet, Jr.	6-4, 6-1
1972	Edmund Swanberg Charles Baird	George Schmid Robert Baldwin	6-3, 7-5
1973	Edmund Swanberg Charles Baird	L. B. Andrus J. L. Dugan	6-2, 6-2
1974	Edmund Swanberg Charles Baird	George Harrison Richard K. Hebard	6-4, 3-6, 6-3
1975	Edmund Swanberg Charles Baird	George Schmid A. E. Muth	6-1, 6-4
1976	Charles Baird Roger Lankenau	A. E. Muth George Schmid	6-3, 6-1
1977	Charles Baird Roger Lankenau	Eric Yeiser-St. J. Bain	6-4, 6-3

National Girls' Doubles

Year	Winners	Runners-up	Score
1973	Lisa Hall Joan Albaugh	Nancy Baird Janet deCamp	6-3, 2-6, 13-11

National Boys' Doubles

Year	Winners	Runners-up	Score
1963	William de Saussure IV Geoffrey Nixon	Michael Brooks Philip Davis	6-0, 6-1
1964	William de Saussure IV Geoffrey Nixon	Rawle Deland, Jr. John Lowman	4-6, 6-4, 6-1
1965	William de Saussure IV Geoffrey Nixon	Rawle Deland, Jr. John Lowman	6-2, 7-5
1966	Rawle Deland, Jr. John Lowman	Charles Saacke Sidney N. Sweet	6-4, 6-3
1967	Charles Saacke, Jr. Richard Blossom	Rawle Deland, Jr. John Lowman	6-4, 4-6, 6-2
1968	Chip Baird Steve Baird	Clayton Auxford H. Lankenau	6-3, 2-6, 6-1
1968	Charles Baird, Jr. Stephen Baird	Clayton Auxford H. Lankenau	6-3, 2-6, 6-1
1969	Charles Baird, Jr. Stephen Baird	H. Lankenau George Krieger	6-2, 6-1
1970	Charles Baird, Jr. George Krieger	Matthew Tekulsky Richard Maier	6-4, 9-7
1971	Charles Baird, Jr. George Krieger	Jay Edwards William Griffin	4-6, 7-5, 6-4
1972	Charles Baird, Jr. James Hartmann	T. Edwards M. Griffen	6-1, 6-3
1973	Thomas Bell Harrison Lauer	T. Manobianco W. Csipkay	6-0, 8-6
1975	Thomas Bell Harrison Lauer	Bill Hammer Kent Pierce	N/A
1976	Rooney Crowley Greg Moore	Jeff Fleitman Sol Hauptman	7-6, 6-4, 4-6, 6-4
1977	Peter Henderson John Quinn	John Mangan, Jr. Tom McEvoy	6-1, 6-3, 3-6, **7-5**

National Men's Singles (discontinued 1938)

Year	Winners	Runners-up	Score
1935	C. E. Grafmueller	Richard G. Newell	6-1, 6-2, 6-2
1936	C. E. Grafmueller	Richard G. Newell	6-3, 6-2, 6-0
1937	Charles M. O'Hearn	Richard G. Newell	6-0, 6-2, 6-3

National Women's Singles (discontinued 1938)

Year	Winners	Runners-up	Score
1935	Mrs. Henry B. Eaton	Mrs. Edward Raymond (Sr.)	6-4, 6-3
1936	Mrs. T. Edmund Beck	Mrs. Henry B. Eaton	9-7, 7-5
1937	Mrs. Percival S. Fuller	Miss Eugenie Thebaud	6-3, 6-4

National Senior Veterans' Men's Doubles (age 60 or over)

1969	Walter Frese George Holloway	John Cookman William deSaussure III	8-6, 6-2
1970	John Cookman Mansfield Sprague	William Miller Gregory Prince	6-4, 6-4

1971	William Miller	Walter Frese	4-6, 6-2, 7-5
	Gregory Prince	George Holloway	
1972	Walter Frese	Mansfield Sprague	1-6, 6-4, 8-6
	Kenneth LaVine	John Cookman	
1973	Mansfield Sprague	Walter Frese	6-4, 4-6, 7-5
	Hugh Lynch	Charles Bucher	
1974	Walter Frese	Mansfield Sprague	6-3, 10-8
	Kenneth LaVine	Hugh Lynch	
1975	Charles Bucher	Mansfield Sprague	6-3, 1-6, 6-4
	Robert Reade	Hugh Lynch	
1976	Brent Baxter	Walter Frese	6-3, 7-6
	Philip Osborne	John Gillespie	
1977	Richard Hebard	Brent Baxter	3-6, 7-5, 6-1
	George Lowman	Philip Osborne	

National Senior Women's Doubles (age 50 or over)

Year	Winners	Runners-up	Score
1971	Mrs. S. Warren Lee	Mrs. William Symmers	6-2, 6-2
	Mrs. Clair Hesseltine	Mrs. Clifford Sutter	
1972	Mrs. S. Warren Lee	Mrs. Walter Mahony	6-2, 6-4
	Mrs. Clair Hesseltine	Mrs. Daniel Badger	
1973	Mrs. Barbara Wood	Mrs. Clifford Sutter	6-0, 6-1
	Mrs. Jean Selvig	Mrs. William Symmers	
1974	Mrs. Charles Stanton	Mrs. Jean Selvig	6-2, 6-3
	Mrs. Oden Cox	Mrs. Sally Norris	
1975	Do Deland	Barbara Kauffman	6-3, 3-6,
	Mrs. E. W. McIllwaine	Mrs. William Symmers	11-9
1976	Mrs. Oden Cox	Barbara Kauffman	6-3, 6-4
	Mrs. Jean Selvig	Mrs. Charles Stanton	
1977	Barbara Kauffman	Mrs. Oden Cox	6-3, 7-5
	Mrs. Charles Stanton	Mrs. Jean Selvig	

National Men's 45's Doubles

Year	Winners	Runners-up	Score
1973	Bradley Drowne	Roger Lankenau	6-4, 4-6, 8-6,
	Donald Miller	Charles Baird	6-4
1974	Roger Lankenau	William Cooper	6-4, 6-2, 6-3
	Charles Baird	Leo Fornero	
1975	Roger Lankenau	Donald Macrae	4-6, 6-1
	Charles Baird	Donald Miller	6-3, 6-2
1976	Donald Miller	Roger Lankenau	7-5, 3-6, 6-1,
	Richard Squires	Charles Baird	7-5
1977	Roger Lankenau	Donald Macrae	7-6, 3-7, 6-4,
	Charles Baird	Mike North	6-4

National Junior Men's Doubles

Year	Winners	Runners-up	Score
1975	Chip Dyer	Thomas Bell	3-6, 7-6, 2-6,
	Ken Walker	Harrison Lauer	7-6, 6-4
1976	Jeff Fleitman	Bill Hammer	6-2, 6-3, 5-7,
	Sol Hauptman	Kent Pierce	6-1